THE NEWSPAPER
ITS MAKING AND ITS MEANING

THE NEWSPAPER

ITS MAKING
AND ITS MEANING

BY

MEMBERS OF THE STAFF OF

THE NEW YORK TIMES

With an Introduction by Dr. John E. Wade
SUPERINTENDENT OF SCHOOLS, NEW YORK CITY

NEW YORK
CHARLES SCRIBNER'S SONS
1945

FOREWORD

IN A WORLD which is changing so rapidly, textbooks of history are of little value in keeping our students informed as to social changes and the way we are going. It is only through the current news, accurately and intelligently presented, that our students can be kept prepared for the changes that are going on.

Because the newspapers have become such indispensable sources of information of all kinds, and because the making and meaning of newspapers is of vital concern to teachers as well as to students, the Board of Education of the City of New York welcomed the opportunity of affording a selected group of teachers the chance of hearing from members of the staff of *The New York Times* how that paper is planned, edited and published.

The teachers who were privileged to attend the course of lectures in Times Hall in the spring of 1945 learned from eminently qualified members of *The Times* staff how a great daily newspaper assembles news reports from all over the world and how public opinion may be guided by editorial interpretations of the significance of the news. I think I may say that never before has any group had the opportunity to hear such a full and frank discussion of the problems of making a newspaper by men who have spent their lives in this work.

The lectures given by *The New York Times* have been especially successful in linking the schools with the newspaper, in stimulating the thinking of teachers and in stressing the place and importance of a free press in safeguarding our democratic ideals and institutions. Schools have the obligation to prepare young people to exercise their responsibility as citizens of a world community. In this training the press furnishes the background necessary for making intelligent decisions upon contemporary affairs. Public education and an intelligent and free press working in harmonious cooperation are basic instrumentalities for the preservation and the progress of democracy.

The workshop which followed the series of lectures was planned to help the teacher in the use of the newspaper as a supplementary teaching resource. The workshop material forms a part of this volume.

I am, therefore, greatly indebted to *The Times* which conceived the idea of presenting this series as a public service.

I wish, also, to express my appreciation to Dr. Jacob Greenberg, Associate Superintendent of Schools, for incorporating the series in our in-service program; to Mr. Isaac Bildersee who directed the workshop, and to the five hundred teachers and supervisors who attended.

It is my hope that those who were privileged to attend will share with others the inspiration and the information gained. I also trust *The New York Times* may find it possible to continue this unique experiment so that more of our teachers may enjoy the enriching experience which grows out of such cooperative effort.

JOHN E. WADE

CONTENTS

INTRODUCTION

WHEN THE COURSE of lectures on "The Newspaper, Its Making and Its Meaning" was planned by *The New York Times* in cooperation with the New York City Board of Education, the objective was to explain the processes of gathering and presenting the news as seen by the men and women who cover, write and edit it. The emphasis was to be on practice rather than on theory. To this end it was arranged that each field of operations would be discussed by a man or woman with extensive experience in that field. So, for example, the Managing Editor was chosen to describe his own work. The Sunday Editor was given the assignment of discussing the problems of editing the Sunday Magazine and special feature sections. The head of the Washington Bureau was asked to explain the work of that bureau. Foreign, national and local correspondents were called upon to tell of the work in their fields, based on their own experience. A former drama critic talked about covering the theaters, and the military editor dealt with the difficulties in his special field. Finally the Publisher discussed the problems and responsibilities of the man who, in the final analysis, decides the policies of *The Times* and sees that they are carried out.

These lectures, now printed in book form, were given in Times Hall in the spring of 1945. They were followed by question and answer periods under the chairmanship of the moderator, Mr. Nicholas Roosevelt of *The Times* staff. Throughout the following pages there runs a common and consistently recurring theme—that the pursuit and presentation of news requires not only great alertness but also the highest standards of honesty, integrity, accuracy and fair play.

In 1901, upon the occasion of the fiftieth anniversary of

the founding of *The New York Times,* on the editorial page appeared this statement:

"The relation of mutual respect and confidence between a newspaper and its readers is its chief asset, all that is precious in its good will. *The Times* will keep faith with its readers in everything it does, to print prompt, adequate, trustworthy news reports, and in its editorial columns to give them the best judgments it can form."

That *The Times* has, throughout the years, kept the faith of the founders will be apparent to the readers of the following pages. *The Times* believes that the high principles of journalism set forth in this volume have not only contributed to the preeminence of *The New York Times* in the field of journalism but also have served as a guide and inspiration to a growing number of editors and publishers in this country and abroad. It welcomes the publication of these accounts of its own activities by members of its own staff because it believes that it is helpful for the public—and especially for the teachers of a great city like New York—to have a clearer understanding of the problems and responsibilities of making a great newspaper. It also welcomes the recommendations of the school teachers embodied in the report of the workshops outlining many ways in which newspapers can be integrated into the work of the school.

The New York Times is indebted to Mr. Robert E. Garst for the preparation and editing of this volume.

CHAPTER ONE

THE ORGANIZATION OF A NEWSPAPER

By Edwin L. James

Managing Editor of The New York Times since 1932, formerly of the Baltimore Sun, war correspondent and chief European correspondent of The Times.

IN THIS SERIES of discussions of the use of the newspaper in the classroom, it has seemed well to begin by describing to you how a newspaper is made—how it comes into being day by day, year after year. For that purpose I will deal with *The New York Times*. The process on all newspapers is a comparable one.

On a Wednesday afternoon tomorrow morning's *New York Times* is not yet born; it is in the making. Friday it will have done its job. But tomorrow it is alive. Thursday morning's newspaper will be current history. It will be the record of the dreams and hopes and accomplishments of untold millions in many lands—and of their disappointments.

From the battlefields of Europe and of the Pacific, from countries around the globe, from all the States of our Union, from all the boroughs of our city it will tell what has happened in the lives and fortunes of more millions of people than one may count.

And if on Friday it is said that Thursday's paper is dead, that is only another way of saying that on Friday morning there will be another paper with the story of what happened in the world Thursday. And thus it goes every day, this story of mankind.

Should you go over to Forty-third Street tonight at 11 o'clock and wait there until 4:30 in the morning, you would see come out of the building some 250,000 pounds of paper. Upon it there will be 4,000 pounds of ink—125 tons of paper with two tons of ink on it.

Over the counters where work the mailers and hustlers you will see the flow of bundles of papers. There it is, being hastened into trucks which hurry off on their way to your breakfast tables and to readers in the forty-eight States of the United States and to a score or more of foreign countries.

To put that two tons of ink on 125 tons of paper to produce 500,000 copies of *The New York Times* required the work of some 3,500 men and women, each doing an appointed task in a very complicated machine.

Take the paper which will be used tonight. Two hundred rolls of three-quarters of a ton each—five carloads of paper. Where did it come from?

Up in the forests of Ontario there is a town of some 4,000 people built just to house the people and the mills which make this paper. There are the mills whose wheels are turned by power obtained from harnessing a river, there are churches, there is a school, there are stores and paved streets and sewers—all put there in the midst of a forest of more than 5,000 square miles allocated by the government of Ontario for this purpose, bigger than the State of Connecticut. It is virtually a perpetual supply, for each acre is cut on a scientific schedule under which that acre will be ready with grown trees before it is reached again. That is where the paper comes from.

If you would pile those bundles of completed papers on each other, they would make five stacks as high as the Empire State Building. Were the papers undone and stretched out page to page tomorrow's edition would reach from New York to Los Angeles. If you would cut those papers into one-column strips, tomorrow's edition would encircle the globe. If it happened to be a Saturday night and we were dealing with Sunday's *New York Times* you could multiply all these figures by five.

But it is more than paper.

It is what is on that paper that counts.

But before going into that, let us trace quickly the mechanical processes by which the finished paper reaches the counters on Forty-third Street.

Those papers have come directly, in pre-counted piles, from the presses. Now it has always seemed to me that a modern newspaper press is the most marvelous piece of machinery in existence. There are twenty-one of them there in the basement of *The Times* building. One high-speed press will deliver 50,000 eighty-page papers, completely printed, folded and counted, in one hour. Through them the paper runs at a speed of more than 200 feet a minute and at that speed the plates make their impression accurately and indeed with complete precision. As a roll of paper reaches its end, an automatic paster functions, and without loss of speed a new roll begins its way through those complicated machines without loss of time. That is something at which I never cease to marvel each time I see it and I have seen it quite a few times.

Now the presses print by bringing the paper into contact with rollers bearing plates, two of them bolted to the circumference of a roller, eight to a roller, and each plate printing one page of the newspaper. The plates weigh fifty pounds apiece, and each night there are cast about 2,000 plates. If each press produces a complete paper, it is obvious that each press must have a set of plates carrying each page of the paper. Then, when you consider that there are three or more editions each night and many corrections made on individual pages, you will see the need for the multiplicity of plates.

Going a step backwards—where do the plates come from? They are moulded in the stereotype room in what are called "boxes." Into each of these boxes, a matrix is fixed with great precision and molten metal is sprayed and fixed against the matrix and in less time than it takes to tell it the "boxes" release the finished plates which are trimmed for the removal of excess metal around the edges and bolted to the rollers of the presses.

Now what are the mats? Up in the composing room, six floors above the press room, matrices which are very much like heavy papier-mâché sheets, each the size of a page, have been pressed down against forms each containing the type for one page, under a pressure of 2,200 pounds to the square inch. There comes out of the mat machine a matrix containing an exact reproduction of the page of type. The mats go down a chute to the stereotype room for the making of the plates from which the paper is printed.

The forms from which the mats are made contain, of course, the type set by the composing room staff. Here again one sees the operation of another machine of astonishing complexity—the linotype. All of the news type, including the headlines, are set on these machines. Each printer has a "take" of copy at a time. By pressing the keys on a keyboard similar to that of a typewriter, he causes moulds, each carrying a letter mould, to fall into lines two inches long—the width of a column. As a line is completed, molten metal is shoved against it, making a reproduction of the line. When a "take" is completed by a printer, it is carried to a "stone" where the different takes of a story, which have been identified through markings by the "copy-cutter," are assembled into the completed story.

This type is placed in the forms through the direction of make-up editors. When the page has been filled by news stories and advertising, the form is locked by screwing down pressure wedges and when this has been done it is ready for the mat-making machine.

We have now traced the material in the paper back to the news room, for it is from the news room that the copy goes to the composing room and then through the different processes I have described, perhaps too briefly.

I expect we have reached the stage which interests you most.

Let us take a look at the news room, going from east to west. It fills the third floor of *The Times* building and overflows onto other floors. In the east end we have the copy desks. There is the telegraph desk, the cable desk and the local desk, each handling the news its name implies. There is also a special desk for the handling of amusement, society and obituary news, and the sports department has its separate desk. In all there are some sixty copyreaders.

To the south of the copy desks is what is known as the "bullpen." The "bullpen" contains the desks of the Night Managing Editor and his assistants. Next, running along Forty-third Street, is the office of the City Editor and his assistants. Next to that is an enclosure where are the desks of the assistant managing editors, secretaries and mail clerks, and beyond that the office of the Managing Editor.

Out from this series of desks is a wide open space devoted to reporters. In all departments *The Times* has some 150 reporters. Somewhat more than half of them work in this large room. Further to the west there is the sports department, offices of various departments, such as society, drama, movie and so forth, followed by the syndicate room, given over to the supplying of *The Times* news to some twenty subscribing papers. At the end of the floor is the important morgue, where are filed millions on millions of clippings about persons and events.

Back of the copy desks is the transmission room into which

flow daily hundreds of thousands of words from all parts of the country, from all parts of the world.

Into this news machine comes more than 1,000,000 words a day. Of this amount we print some 125,000 words a day. The choice of that 125,000 words to print represents a complicated process which produces *The New York Times* and also 99.9 per cent of all the arguments about making a paper.

It is often asked where a million words a day come from—and I shall try to tell you. The most prolific source is The Associated Press, running over 100,000 words a day. Next would come The United Press with perhaps 70,000 words. In all, *The Times* gets the services of nineteen news agencies. Some of them, like Reuter's, the Canadian Press, the North American Newspaper Alliance, supply a goodly amount of what we call "copy." Others of a more special nature, like the Religious News Service, Aneta, the Netherlands News Agency, the Overseas News Agency, and so on, produce less—but it all adds up.

I have not yet mentioned the services of *The New York Times*. Our biggest bureau out of town is the Washington bureau. Here Mr. Arthur Krock has a staff of eighteen reporters in the largest bureau of an individual newspaper in the national capital. The file of news copy from our Washington bureau will vary a good deal depending on news developments in the executive and legislative branches of the government. But it runs into many thousands of words each night. You are to have the benefit of a description by Mr. Krock of the work of his bureau. Of course, we have a bureau at Albany, seat of the State's government.

The Times maintains an office in Philadelphia to cover the news of that city in particular and of Pennsylvania in general. It has a bureau in Chicago to gather news of the Middle West, a bureau in Boston to get the news of New England and a Pacific Coast Bureau in San Francisco.

In addition, we have some 400 correspondents located in

all the important cities of the country. Those correspondents are in general men who hold responsible positions on local newspapers and who are permitted to use the material of their papers in shaping their correspondence for *The Times*.

Then there is the foreign service of *The New York Times,* of which we are proud. Before the outbreak of the war, the foreign service of *The Times* was far and away the most complete and extensive of any American newspaper. We maintained correspondents in all the important capitals of the world and in a number of them maintained bureaus with three, four or five active correspondents. Of course, the war interfered a good deal with that. We have not got offices now in Tokyo or Berlin or in Vienna or in a lot of other places where we used to have them.

We do now have correspondents in London, in Paris, in Turkey, in Rome, in Moscow, in Cairo, in Stockholm, in all of the South American countries, in Mexico, in Australia, in New Zealand, in Canada, in Ireland, in Spain, in Switzerland, in fact, everywhere it is practical to have them.

But, of course, nowadays attention on foreign news is focused on war news. We have some thirty war correspondents in Europe and in the Pacific. We have as many as the military and naval authorities will permit us to have. In France we have seven war correspondents and we will have more when we are permitted. In the Pacific we have seven and will have more when we may.

We publish more war news than any other newspaper. We think it is pretty good. You have certainly read in the war years the dispatches of Raymond Daniell and his crew in London. You have read the front dispatches from that veteran, Hal Denny, from Drew Middleton, from Clifton Daniel, from Gene Currivan, from Fred Graham, from James MacDonald, from David Anderson. You have read the descriptions by Herbert Matthews and Milton Bracker, of the fighting in Africa, in Sicily and in Italy. You have certainly followed the articles from Dan Brigham, in the European listening post of Berne, of George Axellson in Stockholm and William Lawrence in Moscow. Joe Levy has been doing his best under many handicaps in Turkey while Cyrus Sulzberger, who is our chief foreign correspondent, covered brilliantly the German conquest of the Balkans and since then has been doing good work from the Near East observation post of Cairo. Harold Callender is doing an outstanding job in picturing the struggles of France to re-find herself.

I know you have followed Foster Hailey in the Pacific. You have noted the good work of Bob Trumbull with the fleet and of George Horne. Kluckhohn, Lindesay Parrott and George Jones did an outstanding job of covering MacArthur's return to Manila. We now have plans under way for a larger coverage of the final defeat of Japan through a bureau established at Nimitz's new headquarters in the Western Pacific under the direction of Bruce Rae, one of our assistant managing editors.

We mourn Robert Post who did not return from a bombing expedition over Germany and Barney Darnton who was killed in New Guinea. Kluckhohn, Parrott, Denny and Johnston have been wounded.

These men work under many hardships, besides those of personal danger, which they share with the soldiers. Thirty American war correspondents have been killed since hostilities started. They work against time. They know that the best story in the world is no good until it reaches the editor's desk. Transmission delays to them are torture when they know about them and often they do not know their dispatches are delayed. Failure of wireless transmission which cannot be foreseen often occurs. Denny planned for weeks to get into Paris on the first day and to splurge on the story. He manipulated things to go into the French capital with General Le Clerc's armored division. He didn't sleep for forty-eight hours to file what he regarded as one of the big stories of his lifetime. But some general ordered Press Wireless's portable station moved the day before and there was no transmission for two days. It nearly broke his heart.

On a tip from the Army, we flew Clint Green from Pearl Harbor to Saipan the day before the first B-29 raid on Tokyo. The day of the raid the Army transmission from Saipan went out of order. Of course, we got the story from Washington but all of Green's dispatch has not reached us yet. Foster Hailey left San Francisco on a fast cruiser for the Attu show and while the island was being taken he was right there off shore. He thought he was putting his story on a destroyer to be taken to the radio mast of Dutch Harbor. The Lord only knows how it happened, but his story went to Pearl Harbor by ship, from Pearl Harbor to Washington by mail and we got it seventeen days late.

These are just little things that can happen to a war correspondent.

But, all in all, we get a lot of words from them. We print about forty columns a day of war news. And in this connection should be mentioned the outstanding work of our military editor, Hanson Baldwin.

While the lads at the front and correspondents across the country have been working, the local staff has been busy. In column length there is less local news printed now than when there was not a war on, yet it has to be covered and is covered. In addition to the staff of local reporters, who frequently are sent on out-of-town assignments, there are many departments under the general watchful eye of the City Editor. There is the Wall Street bureau which, of course, handles financial news. There is the business news department, the drama department, the movie department, the radio department, the home page department, the music department, the society department, the religious department, and so on. The coverage of suburban news is also under the direction of the City Editor.

The city staff works both in the day and at night—which is only another way of saying that there are stories to be covered in the daytime and stories to be covered at night. Reporters on day assignments report to the City Editor if they have finished in time. There is a consultation between the City Editor and the Night City Editor at which strings are tied together and it becomes the job of the Night City Editor to fit the best of the product of the city staff into the space allotted for local news.

The editorial page is run quite separately from the news columns—as it should be. That is where we express our opinions; our news columns are objective. The editorial page, made up generally of four columns of editorials, a special column by Mr. Krock or Mrs. Anne O'Hare McCormick and two or three columns of letters to the editor, is, of course, in charge of Mr. Charles Merz, the editor of *The Times*. It is put together in the composing room by a special editorial make-up man and always runs in the same relative location in the paper. It carries no news stories. Mr. Merz has his own staff of editorial writers and frequently he calls on the ability of a reporter who is especially familiar with a subject he wishes discussed.

I have tried, then, to give you an idea of the source of our million words a day.

All those words are sorted as they come in, some of them during the daytime, for the different desks which will handle them. Much of this preliminary work has been done when the copy desks start to work around 5 o'clock. All of the words from one front, all of the words on one event, are put into folders ready for the head of the desk when he grapples with his problem each night.

Neil MacNeil, assistant night managing editor, will talk to you on the details of putting the paper to bed. I will touch, therefore, only lightly on the processing of this copy. The head of the desk estimates the relative value of a given story and decides on its length. He then hands it to a copyreader whose task is to edit the material against mistakes of the writer, against mistakes in transmission, against libel dangers, against abrogation of rules of good taste. He has also to cut it into the allotted length and to write the headlines for it.

The Night Managing Editor and his crew receive brief summaries of all leading stories and from that information plan the first page and the size of the heads on the first page. It is the task of the make-up editors, working on both the news floor and the composing room floor, to carry out the instructions of the Night Managing Editor, who is the nearest person to a czar of all the people engaged in making the paper. This is true because his decisions must be made quickly. Less damage may be done by a bad decision which may be corrected in the next edition than by a slow one which may throw the whole production of the paper out of gear; it works in a way that often makes minutes of immense importance.

The first edition goes to press at 11 o'clock. That means it must close in the composing room twenty minutes earlier. By "closing" is meant the completion of all the forms and their dispatch to the mat machines. The second edition must be ready around 1 o'clock and at 2:30 there is a clean-up operation, with opportunity left for insertion of important news which may come in later. Generally, the news operation for the night is finished at 4 o'clock, but when there is expectation of an important news break later than that, the whole business is held until such time as the Night Managing Editor decides from all the factors involved that it is not profitable to wait longer.

I am often asked how the news and advertisements are fitted together exactly in the paper. I think I can best explain that by describing an operation which takes place around

5 o'clock every afternoon. I will describe it as a normal operation, and then explain why it is not now precisely normal.

By 5 o'clock an estimate has been obtained from all news departments of the space they require in the next day's paper. This number of columns is added up. Then there is received from the business manager a statement of the number of columns he desires for advertising. This figure is added to the composite news estimate. Then this figure is divided by sixteen, since the size of the paper moves up or down in factors of two pages of eight columns each. If the result of this division is an even number of pages, the answer is easy. But that happens only once in a blue moon—or longer.

Let me illustrate: if news requests amount to 160 columns and the advertising request is 160 columns, that makes 320 columns or a perfect forty-page paper. But let us suppose that the news requests are 155 columns and the advertising requests 170 columns, we have a total of 325 columns. In that case, five columns of ads would be omitted. If the total were within two columns of a perfect paper, we would add two columns of news. And thus get the right answer. As a general thing the advertising suffers more than the news; after all, the operation takes place in the Managing Editor's office.

Perhaps I should add that if the projected paper is over forty-eight pages, the jumps must, for mechanical reasons, be by four pages instead of two and thus the calculation is complicated, but the same general rules hold.

I said this was the normal way of doing it. But these are not normal times. We have paper rationing, and that means that today we have 30 per cent less paper to use than we had in the year 1941, which has been taken as a base. As a result there is an arbitrary quota size each day for the paper. We have cut our news columnage by 30 per cent, making a normal weekday allotment for news 155 columns. The news department takes that amount out of the quota-sized paper and the advertising department gets what is left, subject to later adjustments if there is a big news break. In 1944 we omitted some six million lines of advertising. We printed several million more lines of news than any other newspaper.

I have said nothing about our magnificent Sunday paper. Mr. Markel, the Sunday editor, is to address you on the subject dearest to his heart. People often comment on the size of our Sunday paper and it has been said that it is sinful because a person cannot read it all and still go to church. But, on the other hand, every time something was cut out to make needed adjustments because of the paper shortage it always seemed that what was left out was just what the Lord knows how many people bought the paper for. Indeed the same thing is true with respect to cutting the daily.

The Sunday paper consists of the main sheet, which is approximately a duplication of the daily paper, with the difference that it carries more advertising; the financial and sports sections, which are now run together; the drama section, which contains much more than drama; the real estate and want ad sections, run together; the book review; the most excellent review of the week section, and last, but by no means least, the Sunday magazine, which is surely the best Sunday magazine published by any newspaper. Mr. Markel will tell you all about it and he is right in being proud of it.

As I have said, there is five times as much paper in the Sunday paper than there is in the average daily paper. Its planning and its production is a highly intricate job. The demand for it exceeds today by about 200,000 the number of copies we can print.

So, I have tried to sketch for you the organization and making of *The New York Times*.

Through no fault of mine, I can assure you, this speech is already too long. Yet there are many things in the making of a newspaper which fall outside of the routine mental and mechanical operations. Mr. Sulzberger, the publisher, who has to shoulder most of the headaches, along with much of the credit, for getting out a good newspaper, will surely speak to you of some of those problems. The Managing Editor will be pardoned for mentioning a few of them.

My pet aversion is the charge so often made in the 1,600 letters which reach my office daily that we "suppressed" some piece of news. Now I have told you that we receive 1,000,-000 words a day and publish 125,000 words. Naturally in that 1,000,000 words there is much duplication. If Mr. Churchill makes a sensational speech in the House of Commons, the A. P. will send a story, the U. P. will send a story and our London correspondent will send a story. But a fair estimate of the duplication is 50 per cent. That means we have available every day enough news to print four newspapers with the amount of news we carry. The cutting of the 1,000,000 words to 500,000 covering the duplication is automatic and not difficult; the choice of 125,000 words out of 500,000 is a process of selection. Our principle is objectivity tempered with relativity and nothing else. Yet the application of that principle is a human process and there may be errors. But the process represents no policy. It is just a matter of objective judgment by the Night Managing Editor and his aides. I ought to know; I used to do the job.

Now, of course, in using one-fourth of the material at hand, one is going to omit stories that a lot of people, for reasons good or bad, would like to see printed. And there you have the basis of the charge of "suppression" which comes along every day. The muck-rakers love it. Some of them make a living out of it.

There seems to be in the minds of many critics an idea that every night there is a council headed by Mr. Sulzberger, with a majority of the stockholders of the paper on hand, to decide whether or not a story gets on page one or perhaps does not get in the paper at all. That is bunk. Nothing like that happens. Our Night Managing Editor is free and untrammeled. He plays no favorites. He does what he thinks best; that is why he has his job. He may make a mistake, but if he does it is not for any reason of policy. We have no news policy save objectivity.

And then there is the old cry that you don't print what the public wants. Ladies and gentlemen, if there is any of you who can present a composite picture of what the "public" wants, I will make it worth your while to let me know. Obviously, the "public" which likes the *Daily Worker* is not going to approve of *The New York Times*. Obviously the public which likes *PM* is not going to like *The Herald Tribune*.

Then there is the old chestnut about big advertisers controlling the news. I have been associated with *The New York Times* thirty years as of last January 1. If ever a story has been printed in this paper which would not otherwise have been printed unless an advertiser asked it, I have not heard about it. If there has been a story left out at the demand of an advertiser I have not heard of it. And it couldn't have happened without my having heard of it. So far as I know, we have never had a business manager dumb enough to ask us to do for an advertiser something which otherwise would not have been done. If there be any of you who don't believe that, give me an example and I will be back here before this series is over to debate the matter.

No discussion of newspaper work these days can be complete without a reference to censorship—generally regarded as a prize headache of newspapers. It is always fashionable in some newspaper circles to damn the censorship. There is sometimes justification because sometimes censorship is stupid.

But I believe it to be true that censorship in this war is infinitely more intelligent than censorship in the last war. I was a war correspondent in the last war. I recall the rule banning all mention of American casualties. It was all right to kill a million Germans before breakfast but we could never mention that an American had received a scratch. That, of course, was quite stupid and explained the terrific shock to the country when Pershing's first casualty list of 35,000 came through. I am sure it is being done better today.

In my opinion Byron Price has done a very good job. When I say that Mr. Price has done a good job I am saying that the newspapers have done a good job because the censorship is a voluntary censorship—something which many people in Washington and elsewhere are prone to forget.

Now in saying that censorship has been not so badly done I am talking about wartime censorship. I am talking about the system by which the newspapers agreed not to violate the rules set forth by Mr. Price, by the War Department and by the Navy Department for the protection of military and naval security. That's all the censorship we have and it is enough. If ever it comes to pass that Washington tries to go into the business of peacetime censorship every newspaper reader in the country should get ready to do something about it. Mr. Price tells me he resigns the day the shooting stops. That is when all American censorship should end.

To give a practical punch to that may I say I hope there will be no censorship of the peace conference this time; a great deal of harm was done by the censorship which shrouded the Versailles Conference.

Just a word on the much-discussed subject of freedom of the press. By freedom of the press is generally meant freedom from government control. It is my belief that here is a danger which has been safely passed for a period as long as we can see. The press of the country has rewon its right to be a free press.

That is no platitude. It has not been so long, just a few years, since the press was a matter of grave solicitude in certain quarters in Washington. There were a lot of people in medium-high places who thought something should be done about it. They wanted to be sure, they said, that there was national unity on our prosecution of the war. They had the club all wrapped up in red, white and blue bunting.

But one sees no more of that club now. I know no project afoot in Washington which could be attacked as threatening the freedom of the press. That the press of the country is now out of danger of radical wartime restrictions under consideration once by persons, some of whom were by no means thinking of the war primarily, is due not alone to sober wisdom in Washington but it is due largely to the press itself.

The newspapers of the country have shown that they can cover the news of the war without wet-nursing by the government.

Ladies and gentlemen, to me it is a significant thing that a quarter of a century ago it fell to the lot of this country of ours to bear the leadership in a fight for a freer and peaceable world. And to me it seems doubly significant that, after our lamentable failure then, it is going to fall to our lot to lead again.

In that leadership our free press is no mean factor. If the example of the United States is to be a big factor in shaping the new world, I would offer our free press as Exhibit No. 1. For a free press and a dictator do not exist in the same country.

And what is a free press? What is the guarantee in our Bill of Rights of a free press? Is it just a guarantee to newspaper publishers? The answer is that fundamentally it is much more than that. It is a guarantee to the people. It is not so much a guarantee to publishers that they may print what they please; it is fundamentally a guarantee to the people that they may read what they please.

And what greater gift have we for the peoples of the world than the right to read what they please?

A bit back I touched on the headaches of getting out a

newspaper. I did not belabor them, for they make such an unimportant chapter. What is important is the daily story of the progress of mankind. There is a charm and a lure about that job which is beyond compare. And when was it ever more attractive than now?

As we swing into 1945, the pincers are being closed on Nazi Germany. The job of crushing Hitler should be completed this year. From the West and from the East the war has been carried onto German soil. It may take bloody months to finish but none of us has any doubts about the end. Nemesis is to take rightful toll of Adolf and his gangsters.

There is plenty of news in that.

Over in the Pacific MacArthur is making good on his promise, "I shall return," and the net is being drawn closer and closer on Japan.

There is plenty of news in that.

Another meeting of the Big Three has just been held. And that calls attention to the fact that not only must the war be won, but the peace must be won, too.

Many of you will remember the last time and all of you know about it. How, as the cannon ceased their angry roar there went up from millions in all lands and across the seven seas the cry that it should not happen again. Fate made of Woodrow Wilson the standard bearer of that vast army of hope. You know the story. He brought back the League of Nations, we killed it and we produced nothing in its stead.

And now we have World War II.

That fight is coming again. This time the prospects look better but it will be an important debate. Perhaps whether we have World War III depends on its outcome.

What more absorbing task could a man have than to help tell that story in *The New York Times?* We hope you will be interested in our telling of it and we trust you will see good in having your pupils read our story.

I have tried to give you a general outline of the organization of this newspaper. Other speakers in other sessions will tell more of the interesting details of how we are trying to do a job which we think is as important as any job there is.

When it is all over I am hoping that you will agree with the verdict that the newspaper is the textbook of democracy.

CHAPTER TWO

INTERPRETATION OF THE NEWS AND THE SUNDAY NEWSPAPER

By Lester Markel

Sunday Editor of The New York Times since 1923. Mr. Markel is a graduate of the Columbia School of Journalism. He joined the staff of the New York Tribune in 1914 and was Assistant Managing Editor of that paper when he left to become the Times Sunday Editor.

ON EVERY OCCASION such as this, I am reminded of the story of the drama critic who didn't like the show at all and so reported and then added: "There is this, however, to be said. I saw the play under unfavorable circumstances. The curtain was up." Well, the curtain is up and here I am and I trust you will not think too harshly of my performance.

One of my severest friends and best critics, Mr. James, in his talk last Wednesday, passed his able judgment on our weekly stint. If I were not unduly modest, I would cite his ringing phrase: "our magnificent Sunday paper." Mr. James is as expert an appraiser as he is a fine colleague. Due in a very great degree to his news sagacity and his news imagination, the daily *Times* is, to my mind, a magnificent daily paper. And, in turn, I salute him.

But whether or not my performance is up to scratch, I

assure you the rôle is a good one. A very good one. For the Sunday newspaper offers a great opportunity—the opportunity to inform and so to enlighten and so to guide.

I propose today to tell you about the Sunday newspaper in general and The Sunday *Times* in particular and, in the course of that recital, to indicate, I hope, how the newspaper can be used as a vital factor in education. I propose also to describe how tremendous and how important has become the task of interpretation of the news, which is, to be sure, the concern of the daily paper but, much more so, the concern of the Sunday paper.

You have heard from Mr. James the story of the vast flow of the news; he has pictured for you the huge assignment each day of winnowing it out; of selecting those dispatches and stories that shall be given the play; of insuring, so far as it can be insured, the accuracy of the news report.

The task becomes increasingly difficult. Once upon a time, in the days when life was simpler, when there were no Hitlers and no Hirohitos, no ideologies and no psychopathologies (or at least they were nameless and so unterrifying), in the days when a "directive" was only a signpost and a "level" only a flat surface, in those days the news was fairly obvious; there was no need for reading between the lines.

This was the formula: if a dog bit a man that was not news; if a man bit a dog that *was* news. But these days it is almost as likely that the first will be news as the second. The dog that bites the man may have been trained by saboteurs to spread rabies in our midst. The man who bites the dog may be Herr Schickelgruber and, inasmuch as rug-chewing or dog-biting or similar antics are reported to be almost daily occurrences at Berchtesgaden, that kind of report hardly qualifies even as local intelligence.

But, seriously, the point I am trying to make is this: that the news has become infinitely complex. Think of the huge and pressing questions that have descended upon us! What single mind can comprehend half the issues that confront us on a single day? Hard or soft peace, Dumbarton Oaks, Bretton Woods, communism or capitalism, 60,000,000 jobs or 40,000,000—perplexity piled on perplexity. As Churchill said yesterday, we are entering into a world of imponderables.

Even in normal times the job of reporting, the mere assembling of the facts, is far from easy. You, the reader, are prone to indict the newspapers for what you call inaccuracy. We, the editors, ask you how accurate are *you* in your daily observations, in *your* news reports? Assume that fifty among you were present at an accident. Do you believe that your fifty would report one set of facts or fifty? Do you believe that any two versions of that accident would agree in detail? Even if you do, I don't. Then why do you assume that the gathering of facts from eye-witnesses or parties with axes to grind or logs to roll is a simple job?

Add to this primary difficulty the wartime handicaps— handicaps about which you will hear in the talks that follow— of censorship, of special interests, of special pleadings, and the task becomes truly formidable.

No, the gathering of the news is not easy at any time and in a period of war it encounters confusion plus obscurity plus ambiguity. No longer are the bare facts all the news—or even a considerable part of it. How accurate would be a war story based solely on the communiqués? Or a political article built wholly on what the politicians tell the reporters? Or a biography written according to what only the biographee divulges?

Now I do not mean to argue that factual reporting is out of fashion or that it should be. Far from it. Never was there greater need for guarding against distortion. Herr Goebbels has taught the world, for all time, what can be the crop that rises out of the seeds of fabrication and of fraud. The basic formula set down by Joseph Pulitzer for the reporter still holds—accuracy, terseness, accuracy. I mean only to say that in these days of great issues it is not enough for the newspaper to supply only the facts; it must provide the background also.

I beg you to understand and to grasp the word "background." It is not as simple a process as you think (or as I once thought). I do not propose to indulge in any elaborate exercise in semantics, that glittering and glib and phony science; I shudder at the vocabular acrobatics that take place these days, among Old Dealers as well as New Dealers—in Washington and in New York, too—in the halls of Congress and, pardon me, within the echoing walls of the classroom. Yet I think it important, very important, that this particular definition be set down as clearly as possible.

What is "background"? It is the deeper sense of the news. It places a particular event in the larger flow of events. It is the color, the atmosphere, the human elements that give meaning to a fact. In short, it is setting and sequence and, above all, significance.

There is also a definition by negation that is extremely important. Background—or interpretation—is *not* opinion. "Obviously," you say and I say it, too. But are we sure that all of us, or even most of us, make the difference or are even aware of it?

Frankly, I am doubtful that we are. I know newspaper men who cannot or will not heed the difference—not green novices who try to act like the chaps in "The Front Page," but seemingly seasoned reporters—not tabloid fellows, but full-sized journalists. And, of course, this particular brand of mental myopia is much more prevalent among the readers, especially those of the educated classes and, most especially, among the subscribers to the so-called publications of opinion.

Basically—and I apologize for being so elementary—the difference is this: what you see or verify is news; what you know is background; what you feel is opinion.

To report that Mr. Jones dislikes Mr. Wallace is news; to explain why there is this dislike is background; to remark that you do not blame Mr. Jones for disliking Mr. Wallace is opinion.

To report that the President and General de Gaulle failed to meet is news; to explain why that meeting did not take place is background; to state that the two should have met is opinion.

Seeing and knowing are background. Feeling is opinion. Background is a vital part of the news. It must be included. Opinion is no part of the news whatsoever. It must be outlawed.

In the daily paper, obviously, the primary job is to cover the news—the essential facts, with such interpretation as is needed to make those facts understandable. But there are wartime restrictions on newsprint. And even in days of peace there are limits to the reader's time. And finally there are the limitations of the human mind to grasp. Thus it is impossible in the daily newspaper, voluminous as it is, to supply all the background of current affairs.

I often wonder how much of the paper is read by the average reader—that mythical, robot-like person created by the pollsters and the chart-makers, with four and a quarter leisure hours a day, a life expectancy of sixty-odd years and two and a half children. Does he spend an hour on his morning newspaper or half an hour, or what? But whatever it may be, this is certain: there is neither the space to provide all the background nor the time to absorb it.

We newspaper editors are likely to assume too easily that most people read most of the paper every day. This is false. And even if it were true, the necessarily disjointed manner in which a running story reaches the reader leaves a vagueness in his mind that needs to be cleared away. The task of the Sunday newspaper is to clear away this vagueness, to provide sign-posts to the news and to illuminate the milestones of events.

As I say this, it occurs to me that your assignment and ours are not unlike. Your task, so far as the teaching of current history is concerned is to a large degree this task of interpretation and of evaluation. And that, surely, is our task, too.

I shall try now to define that job as we see it and to describe, physically, and if you will permit me the word, spiritually, the Sunday newspaper. I am speaking of the Sunday newspaper in general, but if, now and then, I illustrate my points by some reference to The Sunday *Times* you will understand, I am sure, that this is wholly accidental and that the resemblance to any editor, living or dead, is purely coincidental.

First, the vital statistics. Each Sunday we print some 800,000 copies of The Sunday *Times;* of these approximately 450,000 are distributed in the metropolitan area and some 350,000 go to various parts of the country. If we were not forced because of the newsprint shortage to keep the clamps on circulation, the figure would surely be 900,000 and possibly a million. Those 800,000 copies mean 130 million pages, which should not be laid end to end. Each Sunday we consume approximately 700 tons of paper and 22 tons of ink. Most of all, we print some 250,000 words, which is a sizable amount considering that "Gone With the Wind" ran only 240,000 words more and "Forever Amber," that 900-page historical treatise, runs about the same 250,000.

You wonder who reads it all. This I assure you—everything is read by somebody and woe betide us if we make a mistake.

Our readers are heard from on other scores, too, frequently and emphatically. They have all manner of prescriptions for the Sunday paper. There is a considerable group which thinks we are either (a) too conservative or (b) too radical. There is another group which is convinced that we are biased or venal or actually bought because our articles are not slanted in their direction and are therefore clearly prejudiced.

And then there are the comics. The children, their parents report, miss Dick Tracy, The Gumps and Terry and the Pirates. I have always suspected that the parents miss them, too, but that is beside the point. We tell them we are dedicated to fact and not to fiction and that to print non-news features is to take away space from the news—and news space is at a premium these days. But I am sure they are unpersuaded, because they are convinced that the life and times of Flat-top or of Little Orphan Annie are more important than the doings of Churchill or Nimitz.

And there are others. For example, the ardent reader who suggested recently that we leave one column blank alongside each column of radio program because he wanted to jot down his impressions of the broadcasters and file them in his scrap book. Or the teacher who thought the review section so valuable that she wanted to tack up both sides at once, so she suggested that we print it only on one side. Or the old chap in the soldiers' home out West who wrote us that he finished reading the Sunday Times on Wednesday night and he didn't have anything to read for the rest of the week and so he was suggesting that we put out another Sunday paper on Thursday!

If the editor were to try to please all his readers or even a tenth of them he would find himself in a completely and constantly dizzy state. Therefore the best he can do is to follow his own judgment and his own news instinct, printing what appeals to him and what informs him and letting the chips fall where they may. And keeping in mind constantly Mark Twain's admonition: "Always do right. This will gratify some people and astonish the rest."

So that, ladies and gentlemen, is why we cannot imitate four Hawaiians, or four Hearsts, or four McCormicks—and I don't mean Anne O'Hare. As for what we *do* do, I shall try to tell you.

I begin with the organization that produces the Sunday

paper. The Sunday department is set up separately from the news organization; we have a staff of our own, even though we often call upon Mr. James's staff for considerable help in the way of words and sinew. The strictly news sections of the Sunday paper—the main news section, the sports, the financial and the real estate sections—are developed by the news department. The other sections, the so-called news feature sections—the magazine, the book review, the review of the week, the drama sections—are the concern of the Sunday department.

The ideal Sunday paper, as we see it, consists of these three elements: first, the news of the day—the news of Saturday; second, the background of the news of the week; third, something of permanent value.

Note how those three principles determine the make-up of The Sunday *Times* as it is today. The news of the day is given in the main news and the sports and financial sections. The background of the week's news is provided in the review of the week section. The background in special fields—for drama, motion pictures, the rest of the arts, radio, etcetera—is supplied in the drama section. The news of the week in books and the literary background are furnished in the book review. The more or less permanent touch is given (at least so we hope) in the magazine and in the book review.

Thus The Sunday *Times* is, as we believe the true Sunday newspaper should be, both a Sunday and a through-the-week paper. Certainly many subscribers put aside such sections as the magazine, book review and review of the week for possible perusal beyond Sunday; whether they ever get around to doing the reading, I do not know; but at least I credit them with excellent intentions.

For each of the special fields there are special departments set up, each operating in its own way under the eye of the Sunday editor. The direct concern of the Sunday department are the two sections based on the general run of the news—the review of the week and the magazine.

The organization for the production of these Sunday sections is not unlike that of the news department. We have reporters, we have correspondents, we have copy desks; we have pied type, we have deadlines, we have headaches.

The process is a threefold one. First, there is the matter of ideas. Second, there is the problem of the execution of those ideas. And, finally, there is the trick of assembling articles and pictures into layouts 'and pages.

Now about ideas. I venture to say that 75 or 80 per cent of the material appearing in the magazine and special sections of the Sunday *Times* is done on assignment, out of ideas that originate in the office. Inasmuch as we hold firmly to the belief that the Sunday *Times,* like the daily *Times,* is primarily a *news*-paper and should be devoted essentially to news and its background, the great source of inspiration for us is the daily paper.

But we differ from the daily paper in this: the job, so far as the daily is concerned, is a job of selection, the selection of 125,000 words out of some 500,000. And that is, as I have said, a man-size job, if ever there was one.

Our job is rather a job of *election*; we have to seek out our material. We are, as it were, the Frank Bucks of journalism; we go out to bring back articles—alive, we hope, but, too often, not.

Ideas, as you doubtless realize, are the most precious commodity in the world. And the longer I edit the more I am convinced that either you have the news instinct or you haven't. If you have it, the daily paper is a gold mine of suggestion; if you haven't, it is a Gobi Desert.

But the best and the brightest idea in the world is valueless unless it is properly carried into effect. Thus the question of choice of writer becomes all important. Often we use members of the news staff—especially in cases in which an idea needs quick handling. Otherwise, particularly in the case of the magazine, we turn to those outside—occasionally to a free lance writer or more often to a recognized authority in the field.

The expert provides a certain amount of difficulty. There are some who are so expert that no average reader can encompass their meaning. The greatest bother, though, is with those who are the near-experts. The real ones are modest and genuinely desirous of making themselves understood; I still recall that the simplest statement of the Einstein theory appeared in *The Times*—and was written by Einstein himself. But the near-expert will never consent to a change in copy or brook anything remotely resembling a suggestion for revision.

The writer for the Sunday newspaper must have a flair for using the language, but he must not let his style overcome him. He must, above all, be complete master of his facts. And like any good reporter, he must have resourcefulness. In that connection I should like to retell for you what I consider a classic story. It concerns Mr. S. J. Woolf, whose work you have seen time and again in *The Times* Magazine.

Mr. Woolf tells how he tried, without success, to break through the barriers set up by George Bernard Shaw's secretaries in an effort to arrange an interview. Finally on July 1 he wrote to Mr. Shaw as follows:

"My dear Mr. Shaw—Years ago I remember you said that the only reason you posed for Rodin was because you felt that it was the one way in which you would gain everlasting fame. That is quite true as far as Europe is concerned, but as for America, with true Shavian modesty, I may say that immortality will not be yours there, until I have drawn you. That is one of the reasons why I came to London—to obtain immortality for you in America. And when you think it will cost you only one-half an hour of time—that is a very small price to pay."

The following morning Mr. Woolf received this letter from Mr. Shaw: "I now have considerable experience as an artist's model; but my terms—about $3,750 an hour—are prohibitive. Also, I shall not be disengaged for at least a year to come."

Whereupon, Mr. Woolf drafted this rejoinder: "My dear Mr. Shaw: Your price for posing is acceptable to me. My price for drawing is the same amount. You do not have to be disengaged while I draw. I am leaving on the eighth. When shall I come? If you could pose this afternoon and sign the drawing today, think what it would mean to the American people to have two vital documents on July 4."

And so Mr. Woolf got the job and the drawing and an outstanding interview. Such is the fruit of resourcefulness.

The third step in the Sunday process is the preparation of the copy for the printer and the laying out of the pages. The manuscripts go through our copy-reading mill—much as they do in the news department. While this has been going on we have been gathering illustrations. That is a department in itself—and a very important one. It fulfills two main functions: the first, for the review section, is the business of watching the daily flow of pictures—and that flow is enormous—keeping in touch with the nation's cartoons and (this is especially vital) planning the war maps; the second, for the magazine and the book review, includes those sources and others, too—galleries, print shops and museums. It is an interesting job and an exacting one.

Finally, there is the assembling of **text** and picture in the pages in the composing room—a matter of make-up which Mr. James has described to you. In the case of the Sunday paper, it is somewhat slower and has to be checked more carefully because once we send a page away it is gone, frozen in copper or in lead for the generations—utterly beyond change. The daily has another edition in which corrections can be made. We must stand or fall on our final okay— and sometimes, I tell you confidentially, we fall. Putting a paper to bed, as the expression goes, is no job for a nurse's aide; it calls for a graduate nurse of long standing. Because often the "form" requires a hot-water bottle or a rub-down and not infrequently a sedative.

But somehow it always comes out—and the show goes on. The larger problems lie in another direction. They are the headaches and the heartaches reserved for those who venture into the realm of prophecy.

Of all hazardous professions, including tight-rope walking, flag-pole sitting and budget balancing, I should say that Sunday editing comes close to being first.

You see we go to press with the magazine on Wednesday. Also we feel it important that we hit topics on the nose or approximately so. Thus, in these days of fast moving events, it takes the seventh son of the seventh son of a Pearson to do anything approximating the job that is required.

I recall a prime example of this kind of thing which took place some years ago. We had a most excellent article on General Obregon. But three days before we appeared on the streets, he was assassinated. And on Sunday, there on the first page, was an eloquent description of Mexico's "greatest living man." All we could do was to explain the time-lag editorially.

On the other hand, I recall the case of Briand in the days when France was moving along in her normal abnormal way. I remember distinctly that headline, "Europe's Man of Peace." But before the magazine could appear, Briand was deposed as Prime Minister. It looked hopeless. But on the Saturday before the fateful Sunday Briand was called on to form a new Cabinet, and so we could not have had a timelier piece.

It is a tribute to us, or more likely to our tremendous luck, that I cannot recall a similar incident in the past few years. As I say this, I have my fingers crossed about next Sunday's magazine.

But this is all theory. Let us now see how it is applied; let me tell you how next Sunday's paper is being prepared. I shall speak of the review section and the magazine because they are the sections which best illustrate how we function and because they are sections based on the kind of "background" that has been the text for this talk.

The review section is designed to perform a twofold service: the first two pages are devoted to a summary of the news of the week, done in proper perspective and with the needed background. The pages that follow are given to articles assembled from all over the world, to provide the interpretation.

The summary is designed to pull together the threads of events; to link up disconnected dispatches; in short, to provide a sort of "Outline of History" of the week. But it is much more than a rewrite of the daily news. A great deal of research work goes into it, in an effort to enrich it, both in the way of fact and of color.

That research work is a sort of treasure hunt. Each day, out of the leads we find in the daily paper, we seek out additional facts and atmosphere to provide a rounded and graphic picture.

Some of that material we find in our own files and morgue and through sources available in the city. Some of it is the result of queries sent abroad or to our men in Washington or throughout the country, who supply to us, by wireless or telegraph, memorandums which are incorporated into the summary.

The summary staff consists of five members. The accepted formula for this kind of work on the news weeklies is that a leg-man or, more likely, a leg-woman shall do the research and the writer polish up the facts and add the adjectives. We believe that the writer shall do his own research and search out his own background material, because we think a unity and balance are thus achieved greater than is likely under the other system.

The work begins on Tuesday morning and continues through Saturday afternoon. Thus our summary is only three hours or so behind the main news section in timeliness. And many were the uncomfortable Saturdays Herr Hitler used to give us. For some reason or other, his invasions or coups or purges were always timed for Saturday morning, which meant a furious scrambling in the Sunday department and often a complete rearrangement of our plans. But that menace, among other Hitler menaces, is now removed.

The interpretative articles which, with the editorial page and the education and science departments, comprise the rest of the section, are assembled from three sources: by cable or wireless from *The Times* correspondents throughout the world; by leased wire from members of our Washington bureau; and by telegraph from a staff of editorial correspondents in various parts of the country. Among these articles are the weekly contributions of Mr. James and Mr. Krock; these have won large laurels and a very wide audience.

We shift articles and layouts, of course, up to Saturday afternoon, but inasmuch as these pieces require a considerable amount of research and background they call for time; and so our guesses have to be better than fifty per cent or we are likely to find ourselves in a good-sized hole.

Now let us see how next Sunday's review section (March 4, 1945) is coming along. All this is, of course, completely confidential and I hope there are present no Luce researchers or Winchell Pinkertons.

Yesterday, as we do each Tuesday, we drew up a schedule. Even though Sunday is five days off we try to project ourselves to the week-end. Two sets of orders went out, one to our foreign staff, one to our Washington and domestic correspondents, indicating the nature and the length of the interpretive articles we desire.

These articles will arrive by wireless from our foreign staff and by wire from our Washington and domestic correspondents tomorrow night and Friday night, with the understanding that any new developments will be covered by new leads or inserts through Saturday afternoon.

So this is the way we see the news for next Sunday: (and I trust your memories are short). Here are some of the items on the schedule:

We are hoping to get from Hanson Baldwin a statement of what the Germans are up against in the way of manpower, supplies, morale and what not.

From Clifton Daniel, at SHAEF, an article on the objectives in the present West Front drive.

From Raymond Daniell, in London, a report on Churchill's report on Yalta.

From Sidney Shalett, in Washington, a piece on the rôle of air power in knocking out Japan.

From James B. Reston in Mexico City, an article on where the present conference leaves the Good Neighbor policy.

Domestically, among others, we have ordered these pieces:

An article on the prospect of a miners' strike.

Apropos of the curfew, a piece on the strength of the prohibition movement.

From Washington, an article on the mood and present activities of Congress.

That list is by no means complete but it indicates the way in which we try to build the review closely on the week's news. And that is what I had in mind when I spoke so reverently of the art of prognostication.

The process of getting out the magazine is similar to that of producing the review—1) ideas, 2) execution, 3) presentation. Magazine ideas also flow out of the daily paper, but the effort there is to deal with the long-range news rather than with the immediate news of the week.

We define news in its broadest sense. It includes two categories: one, to which the designation "spot news" might be applied, deals with specific events; the other, which might be called "spread news," deals with the continuing current of events.

To illustrate: the importance of the capture of Iwo to the advance on Japan is spot news for the review; the nature of the Japanese homeland and the large job of conquering it are spread news and something for the magazine. An article on Mr. Wallace's chances of confirmation is a spot news piece for the review; the question of how sacrosanct is the President's right to select his own Cabinet members is a spread news theme for the magazine.

And the difference is much broader than that. Matters discussed at the dinner tables—and in the subways—may never reach the state of being "spot news" but they are certainly "spread news" and of the widest interest—matters, to name a few, such as the state of mind of our returning veterans, the psychology of our teen agers, "modern" education, the home life of our teachers and many more of the same nature—matters that never quite focus into news dispatches but are in their way our most important and pressing issues.

There is another important difference between the sections. The review articles, while they provide background, do not generally contain opinion—or at least the opinions of the writers. In the magazine we publish articles of opinion, provided that—and this is a large proviso—the opinion is important enough to be news. On controversial issues, we make it our policy to present both sides, often in the form of a debate.

Unlike the review, we work far in advance on the magazine, trying to guess what the big news will be a month hence or thereabouts but ready to shift our schedule at a moment's notice. The reason for this lies in the nature of the articles themselves. These are important pieces with a certain literary quality and they cannot be turned out with the speed of news dispatches. Moreover, a good many of our contributors are well-known figures in public life or in letters and you cannot brow-beat them with deadlines the way you can the more humble reporter.

But when a big story breaks we can turn quickly to a writer—or we may have on hand a piece which, with a new lead or introduction, will turn the trick. We use wire and wireless frequently for transmission of magazine articles to give the section the news flavor which we feel is its essence. That is really the secret of our magazine "success" (if any) : to try to see the news ahead, to plan accordingly and to be ready for a quick shift.

In the magazine that was sent to press last night, this kind of shift and our news approach are both demonstrated.

On Thursday, when our make-up started, it looked very much as though the invasion of Iwo—as dramatic a story as any of the war—would be the big news of the week; and the section was laid out accordingly. Then, on Friday, came Eisenhower's newest drive and we shifted the emphasis to the West Front.

Therefore in next Sunday's magazine you will find a lead article describing operations at Supreme Headquarters, especially when a big push is on. That article was received by wireless last night.

Then comes a West Front layout, together with an article describing the sensations of an American soldier on the eve of the new offensive. This also was sent by wireless.

Then the layout on the Pacific, with an article wirelessed direct from the Iwo beachhead.

All these are pieces on the news—"spread" news pieces to complement the "spot" news pieces in the review.

As for the mechanics of producing the magazine, that is done much as the review, with a staff of editors to pass on manuscripts (incidentally, we receive, I should say, some 200 manuscripts a week out of which two or three may be acceptable; but the flow continues—everybody tries to get into the writing act), a staff of copyreaders to prepare the copy for the composing room (and I assure you that a good deal of the copy, even from our top-notchers, needs attention); a staff of make-up people to handle the pages in the composing room.

All this demonstrates how the mind of a Sunday editor works or should work—or maybe shouldn't.

It indicates also, I believe, how the newspaper can be made a vivid textbook for the study of current affairs. May I offer a few thoughts on that score, even though I am sure I could not pass Dr. Greenberg's tests?

First, I suggest that you follow the development of a story day by day in the newspaper. You will find it an absorbing business. You will realize then how each issue can be read as a chapter of the world's annals, to be considered in the light of what has gone before and what is likely to come after it; it is thus revealed to be the true source of contemporary history.

Second, I recommend the acquirement of insight into the news—the art of reading between the lines. You will discover that to be hugely gratifying. You will begin to ask: what is the background of this present event? What is its significance? In its broad sweep the newspaper deals in a single day with many of the great problems that confront the world. In its pages there is a wealth of human drama, there are many facts far stranger than fiction.

Above all, I urge you to mark the difference between news and opinion. For there are too many, who knowing that distinction, are willing to disregard it. They are deeply attached to their biases; they wear them, like wound stripes, on their sleeves, and display them proudly to every passer-by. And it is noteworthy that nine out of ten complaints made to newspapers on the score of bias are not that there is bias shown but that the bias is in the wrong direction.

The handicaps to the approach by reason rather than by emotion are growing—and at an alarming rate. One great difficulty is this: that it is considerably easier to have an opinion than to grasp a fact. And the opinions are there to be had. There are the newspaper exhorters, the for-godsakers, the columnists and the commentators; there are also the radio oracles and the soapbox Sinatras. From all of them it is *so* simple to pick up a smattering of judgment that will pass as thinking.

Thus bias is formed and the barnacles begin attaching themselves to that lumbering ship called public opinion.

I may be prejudiced, but the strident radio voices bother me particularly. Words set in type seem so much calmer, so much more logical than the words that issue from the loud-speakers.

In that connection I am always amused at the assertion that the spoken word will take the place of the printed word, that before long the radio will be the sole source of both news and opinion. Maybe so, but I strongly doubt it.

I firmly believe that even twenty-five years from now people will still be reading as well as listening. Newspapers will continue to exist for a very solid reason: namely, all reading habits are not alike; some people read rapidly, others slowly; some like to read the news in the morning, others in the evening; some like to start with the sports pages, others with the arrival of buyers; some go for comics, others for obituary notices. And so no mechanical device, calling the nation to setting-up news reading at 7:45 every morning, is likely to take the place of the newspaper.

Now I do not underrate the radio. I think it has its great and good uses. It reports with a speed no newspaper can achieve, and so it is invaluable for news bulletin service. It can carry into your home the voices of the leaders of the world. It can entertain you by your fireside—and I speak of chits as well as chats. But it cannot provide for you what the real newspaper provides.

The real newspaper provides the full report, calmly and without fanfare or flourishes. Most of all, it provides perspective—an appraisal of the news made with the kind of judgment and background I have been attempting to describe and without any slant whatsoever.

There are vast blanks in our national information. For example, it is reported that of the 138 million 100 thousand estimated Americans, 138 million have never seen or read the Dumbarton Oaks proposals and 100 million have never read the Atlantic Charter. These are appalling voids when we consider the huge tasks before us—tasks that only informed public opinion can achieve. Upon all educators, whether they work in the schools or in the news rooms, rests the responsibility of clearing away at least some of this dangerous ignorance.

The newspaper can help greatly, I believe, in that endeavor. It is, as I have tried to show, indispensable to the study of current history. For a newspaper is much more than a business; it is surely much more than a medium of entertainment; it is much more even than a purveyor of intelligence. It is a great force for good or for evil, for it holds within itself the means of molding public opinion. And that opinion, if it is to be sound and therefore effective, must be based on an unimpassioned study of unimpassioned facts.

The newspaper offers a challenge and an opportunity—for the teacher as well as for the editor. Used as it should be used, without bias, without fear, without favor, it can be a great instrument of democracy.

Our goals lie in the same direction. It is a privilege to work with you toward achieving them.

CHAPTER THREE

THE GATHERING OF THE NEWS

I

By Arthur Krock

Chief of the Washington Bureau of The New York Times. Mr. Krock began his newspaper career in Louisville, Kentucky, in 1907 and in 1915 became Managing Editor of the Louisville Courier-Journal and the Louisville Times. He was assistant to the President of the New York World from 1923 to 1927 and an editorial writer on The New York Times from 1927 to 1932, when he was made head of the Washington Bureau of The New York Times. He won the Pulitzer Prize in 1935 and again in 1938.

I SHOULD LIKE TO DIVIDE this topic into three parts. And, since ancient you-know-where was similarly divided, perhaps it is appropriate to add that those of you who stay to the end will deserve Caesar's accolade to the Belgae: "Fortissimi sunt."

The three parts are: First, a non-technical and reasonably brief account of the job of gathering the news of Washington; how that differs from usual reporting and requires that the reporters be specialists. Second, suggestions how you can use this reporting for class-room work. Third, what allowances and discounts for the news reports from Washington may be cited by you to your students.

I

As Mr. James has told you, the Washington bureau of *The New York Times* is its largest unit outside the headquarters here. We have had as many as 22 reporters, a number of whom have gone into uniform. At the moment we have 19.

In immediate charge of the assignment of these reporters, and of editing what they turn in, is a managing copy desk of three men. The manager, Mr. Luther Huston, spends his day in seeing that a *Times* man—we have two women reporters also, however—is at the spot where news has broken, is breaking or may break.

I do not mean all news. Our process must be selective, and for several reasons: one, there is not enough newsprint even in days of plenty to publish all the activities of Washington; two, *The New York Times* receives the reports of press associations which attend to routine—stories which speak for themselves and require no special investigation; three, Washington is crowded with publicity-seekers in office whose emanations rarely survive the selective news test and which often cannot be verified.

It is the business of the chief of the bureau and, under him, the managing copy desk to prejudge each day what those events will be that will require special investigation, special knowledge or extended treatment. The most important happenings must also be forecast on the assignment book. But even in this winnowing process the Washington news that is sent to New York for final editing and ultimate selection ranges from 15,000 words on a normal day to 30,000 or more. And when texts abound it has run to 50,000.

Our reporters, as I have said, must be specialists, but also they must be competent narrators of the spontaneous. A man on what we call a beat—for example, all financial and economic departments and bureaus—must be as proficient in writing a story with a life of one day as in following a continuing episode in government. Thus, he must be as quick and accurate an observer of human activity as a police reporter, and also be equipped to deal intelligently and clearly with such a subject as the world refinancing that began at Bretton Woods. And he must have the resource and the industry to rescue legitimate news from its kidnappers in office.

Mr. Catledge, who sits here suppressing with difficulty, I am sure, a speech that will be both witty and wise, has effected many such rescues. But I shall use another illustration—the exclusive publication by this newspaper of all the texts of the drafts of the world security league at Dumbarton Oaks by the major allies.

For reasons that did not seem sound at the time, and were proved by the publication not to be, our authorities forbade textual release of our plan and, as their host, urged delegations from the other countries to follow suit. It was a censorship in restraint of proper public information, in our opinion, and we set out to break it through our reporter on the scene, Mr. James B. Reston.

Some time before, he had ferreted out the identity of a person to whom all the Dumbarton Oaks texts would be made available but who in no sense would be obligated—by pledge, honor, national or international interest—to accept the policy of silence. This fact was overlooked by the government, but not by Mr. Reston.

He persuaded this person that the texts were rightful public property and absolutely essential to the public's daily and final understanding of the problems discussed and disposed of at the conference. He got them, and we published them all.

Rival reporters charged favoritism by our delegation, which was not the case. They accused the British of leaking to Mr. Reston, who had won their admiration when our London correspondent, but the British were not guilty. The source to whom the reporter applied was open to any of his competitors and to the same arguments. It was a good day when we hired him.

Our employment practice is, whenever possible, to hire a reporter for a particular line of government news in which he has already been grounded. But this practice is often relaxed to employ an able, seasoned and experienced gatherer and writer of general news, for such a reporter can soon become a specialist. College training is valuable, particularly when an applicant has majored in English, politics, civics, economics, finance, labor relations or American history. But my judgment is that major credits in English and American history should always accompany those in a special field if a reporter is to come prepared for Washington newsgathering.

Another attribute is peculiarly necessary for this work: a Washington correspondent must keep more rigidly the confidence of news sources, for it is in confidence that much important news is acquired which otherwise would be withheld from the public that has a right to know it. One breach of such faith, and that news source is closed.

The reason a great deal of official information comes in this manner is because the tendency of many high officials is to protect themselves from their errors—less frequently from their misdemeanors—by putting the lid on their subordinates. It is the business of the public newspaper to lift that lid for legitimate and news-worthy revelation. Policy and the standards of newspaper management determine whether the published results are to be unverified gossip and tale-bearing, animated by personal spites and ambitions; or whether these results are to be important and dignified news. You and other readers of newspapers must be the judges whether information not attributed to a specified source is in one category or the other. We strive to assure that Washington news dispatches of this type in *The Times* are in the second category.

Another vigil we keep is against the intrusion in news dispatches of the personal views, political philosophies, likes or dislikes and other prejudices of the reporter or his superiors. Color is admitted to a news story only when it is a fundamental ingredient in the sum of the facts. Adjectives with a slant are deleted if they creep into a story. And if the desk in Washington or in New York decides that the emphasis in a dispatch is too heavy on one factor, so that it suggests—or seems to suggest—any of the personal animations I have listed, the story is ordered rewritten.

I think we have maintained this vigil with success, subject to the human failings which afflict those who engage in all occupations. And it has not been difficult. Our reporters approve as well as comprehend the news standards set by Mr. Ochs. Seldom are they breached: and never, in my experience deliberately by an executive of this newspaper. The same standards govern the headlines and placement of the news, with which, however, the Washington bureau has no connection. What you find plainly labeled facts as contrasted with comment or opinion, are the facts to the best of our ability to discover and present them.

But for a full understanding of the news—especially that from Washington—interpretation and analysis are indispensable. We entrust this essential function to reporters whose knowledge of the subject and devotion to standards have been established. In four of the five articles weekly which appear under my name I attempt to discharge some of this duty, but numerous news dispatches must include interpretation for reasons Mr. Markel has so brilliantly described to you. But, since I sometimes include comment and opinion, these four articles appear on the editorial page and on a Sunday page which carries the same type of material.

The reader, therefore, is on continuous notice that this material, while based on the news and more often than not the vehicle of new factual matter, is an expansion of the formula that controls the news columns.

On the chance it may interest you, I should like to add that my chief purpose in these articles is to clarify and relate to germane activities what the basic news story has described, and to give more pertinent information on the subject if I can acquire it.

The other day, when Mr. Markel managed to be continuously entertaining while he was being continuously informing, he said:

"The point I am trying to make is this: that the news has become infinitely complex. Think of the huge and pressing questions that have descended upon us! What single mind can comprehend half the issues that confront us on a single day? Hard or soft peace, Dumbarton Oaks, Bretton Woods, communism, or capitalism, 60 million jobs or 40 million—perplexity piled on perplexity."

His automatic illustration happened to be topics and events in the news which originate and develop more in Washington than anywhere else in the world. It is our daily business through the medium of reporting to resolve these complexities and obviate these perplexities. I am sure no newspaper task is more difficult, so please bear this in mind when we fail, as we often do.

Back to our news gathering machinery:

Voluntary and mandatory censorship—the latter enforced through statutes by the armed services and the White House, the former enforced by the press itself—have added to the problems of a Washington bureau. And the incidence of war, which has produced these censors, vastly increases the burden. We must now often, as a matter of patriotism, accept an official view of what is publishable and what is not. We must lean backward to suppress news, normally legitimate, which would give aid or comfort to the enemy or imperil the security of the state or individuals. We must, to save news-print, condense what before we had the space to expand. How well the press as a whole has met these obligations I must leave to you.

We must, within the spot news formula, explain the "why" of a story as well as the "who, what, how, when and where." This necessity is most often imposed by the official press conferences.

As these are conducted, the public official is the host. The time and subject matter are controlled by him. Particularly at the White House there is a limit to questioning, even when honestly designed to amplify or clarify what has been stated. News is offered, naturally, with the best possible face on it from the viewpoint of the source. And very often as stated it is misleading, incomplete or dull.

The business of the Washington bureau is to supply the missing essential elements, to balance the misleading or confusing element with the clarifying one, to breathe into the story the life that has been withheld and belongs there. And this must be done in such a way as to leave room for no reasonable charge that the news has been tampered with.

This extra element of the news enables readers to see it in its full perspective and current application, and that distinguishes the specialist's, the Washington correspondent's, reporting from the routine.

His training and information make it possible to keep this element within the formula of the pertinent fact. But we add this element in the daily paper only when it seems to be required for a full understanding of the news. In news articles for the Sunday review section, as Mr. Markel has explained, it is the topmost ingredient of the Washington dispatches. Otherwise, they would merely be a catalogue of what was published throughout the week, and thus a duplication of the material on pages 1 and 2 of Section 4.

What are known as handouts also call often for the specialist's treatment if the reader is not to be imposed on.

Hundreds of them come in daily, many of them duplicates and many out of date. These, with purely personal publicity for officials, are thrown away. Others are amplified or clarified as the necessity requires. Those that tell the full set of facts—and they are the minority—and offer no need or opportunity for extra research are left to the press associations.

The personal puffs of men in office, and most of their speeches that are distributed as handouts, are the work of ghost writers. When I see one of these compositions I think of the story about the man who was walking by a hedge. Behind it he heard a most interesting, brilliant and intelligent conversation in progress. He looked over the hedge and saw that the conversationalists were two dogs—a big greyhound type and an approach to a dachshund. He saw a house beyond the hedge, he rang the door-bell and, when a man appeared, he asked: "Are those your dogs?" "Yes." "I want to congratulate you on the ownership of such remarkable animals. I have listened to what they are saying. Never have I heard sounder arguments or better information." "Oh," said the owner, "you are about the fiftieth victim of a delusion. You see the big dog? Well, he is deaf and dumb. The little dog is a ventriloquist."

Our reporters begin to write their copy in the late afternoons to meet edition time in New York. Their copy is carefully edited in Washington and then re-edited in New York before it gets into the paper. It is forecast by what are called "schedules"—and there are syllabi of what each major story will contain so that the New York editors will know what is coming and plan those parts of the paper into which it will go. Schedules are also the means whereby the editors in New York can make suggestions to change, amplify, reduce or throw away, in conformity with whatever special information they may have on the stories. But policy, in the sense the word is usually employed, does not limit news in *The Times* except that it shall be "fit to print."

I think that is enough—probably too much—about the mechanics and standards of Washington news reporting.

But the machinery is unduly clogged at times—and the official tendency to do this was once very humorously acknowledged by Mr. McNutt, the War Manpower Commissioner. Pressed for a statement on a news development he said "No comment"—the familiar refuge of the bureaucrat at bay. Then he asked solemnly if he could answer "off the record—" that is the other great escapist phrase of Washington. Informed that he could, he cleared his throat and said: "Off the record, no comment."

This cliché is heard so much in the capital that on one occasion Gardner Cowles, Jr., making a radio speech as head of the domestic branch of the OWI, absent-mindedly inquired of the microphone: "May I say now, off the record . . . ?"

II

The second section of my topic is how to use Washington news and expanded articles in the classroom. Permit me, since I cannot deal with all the branches of teaching—knowing nothing about any—to take as an example a class in current events.

Congress assembles early in January, and the President sends to it a message on the state of the Union, containing certain recommendations for legislation; also a message on the budget.

The thorough Washington news report carries all this material textually and describes the steps taken to adopt, reject or modify the President's requests.

Assume that the class, or a section of it, is assigned to follow the progress of a tax bill, or a world security treaty. Each day until action is completed the teacher and the students will find the current history of this enterprise in the daily paper. Each day, therefore, the developments can be recited and discussed—the latter pivoted on the editorial and comment columns devoted to this subject. When the enactment stage has arrived the student will not only know a typical case of history of legislation, but he will know the processes of government in such matters. And he will then be in a position to select some part or all of this for theme purposes.

If a class had been—as doubtless many were—assigned to read the daily reports of the proceedings of Dumbarton Oaks, and to recite and discuss the news of this as it proceeded, the students would have understood the whole great subject of international security in its formative stages. This could easily be linked with an account of what happened at the end of the last war, and with summaries of the differences in plan and method.

In other words, I think the daily newspaper dispatches are textbooks, too, and can be employed as such. Classes in English can study them with profit and learn from their errors, I assure you. And in many branches of education they offer continuing source material.

All this, of course, is obvious to you, and I do not doubt I am suggesting what you do already. So this brings me to a survey of the allowances and discounts which I think teachers should outline to classes in their study of the daily newspaper.

III

Goethe said: "It is much easier to recognize error than to find truth. Error is superficial and may be corrected; truth lies hidden in the depths."

I can only repeat, in conferring with you on means by which to correct our errors to your students, that we try to avoid them with such diligence that I hope most of them are superficial; that when a correction is indicated, and the case for it is even fairly good, we make it; and that we dredge to the best of our ability the depths in which truth dwells.

But the people who collect, write and publish the news are subject to the human limitations which are the origins of error. Their only sound claim to credibility—if you will grant good faith and good intent—is that they are trained to observe, and have been born with or develop that sixth sense which is the instinct for what is news. Like yourselves, they are practitioners of a trade or profession. But, beyond allowing them the status of skilled artisans, you owe them no privilege of immunity from question; and the freedom of the press is not theirs, it is yours and that of the rest of the public.

Therefore, the makers of a newspaper are not free by any law or custom to select and prepare for publication that which they *wish* you to read, to the extent they *wish* you to read it, and to reject all else. Their obligation is to give you as much as space permits of the events of daily life, and to give it to you balanced, straight and fully—whether the product be news, exposition, comment, exhortation or opinion.

This requires the exercise of several sets of professional judgments—up to the ultimate editing at press-time—as to what shall be presented to you, and where and how. And in that exercise error, and even injustice and wrong often appear.

So far as are concerned the news columns for which I am originally responsible, or with which I am familiar, I do not think you need to discount them except in the degree that they are produced by humans, and therefore are fallible as to judgment. So far as the editorials are concerned, you are free to take or leave the opinions expressed and the positions stated, but I do not think you have need to discount this newspaper's exposition, editorials or presentation of supporting facts. These are gathered painstakingly from all available sources. So far as the Sunday review articles from Washington are concerned, they may express a point of view; but it is plainly labeled, and the Sunday editor toils endlessly and with success to make them interpretative and informing. The dispatch of mine which usually appears in the news columns on Wednesday mornings attempts to remain within these same limits.

But in my signed articles on the editorial page and in the Sunday review section, while I express at times opinions which are personal, I carefully mark them as such. These, it seems to me, the reader will evaluate—and the teacher to his students—according to his estimate of the body of the work for accuracy, fairness and penetration into the depths of which Goethe spoke. If he thinks a writer fundamentally deficient in any of these qualities, he should reject all his opinions. If he thinks him reasonably equipped with these qualities, he should still measure the views against the new background offered in their support. And always—this goes for every comment writer and the director of every editorial page—if he finds that generally certain public persons are spared from the criticisms made of others (for the same alleged faults), he should discount the commendation of such persons and look twice at the criticisms.

Distrust of any writer of comment or editorial opinion may come, of course, solely from disagreement with his expressed philosophy or his appraisal of those about whom he writes. But that, too, is the privilege of the free American reader of a free press, and of the free teacher in a free system of education. It should not, and fairly cannot, be extended to the news columns of *The Times,* including those from Washington. If I speak too often of this newspaper, and mostly of its Washington report, please forgive me in the remembrance that such was my topic, and such are the matters on which I know the most of what little I do know.

THE GATHERING OF THE NEWS

II

By Turner Catledge

Assistant Managing Editor of The New York Times. Mr. Catledge entered newspaper work in 1921 and served on various papers in the South until he joined the staff of The New York Times in 1929, serving that paper in Washington and elsewhere. He was with the Chicago Sun from 1941 to 1943. He was appointed Assistant Managing Editor of The New York Times early in 1945.

IN THE ABSENCE OF SOME overwhelming event, such as a foreign war, in which this country is directly involved, the prime news interest of American newspaper readers, and, therefore, of the newspapers who serve them, is here at home. While I do not have statistics immediately at hand to prove the assertion, it is nevertheless a known fact that up until 1940, when it became obvious that we would be drawn into war, the largest amount of news space in the average American newspaper was devoted to local happenings. The second largest amount was given over to state and national events, and a poor third, to foreign news. Up until then by far the greatest percentage of news moving over the wires of the Associated Press and the other news services, was intrastate news, developed for and by, and printed by, newspapers within a given state.

There is hardly need for my reminding you, of course, that

the situation is considerably different today. The principal interest of readers and daily publications is centered now largely upon the foreign scene. Of the "live" news printed daily in *The New York Times*—that is, news dealing with current events and developments—by far the largest proportion today is of overseas origin.

That, I might add, might not hold for the country as a whole, but it will approach the situation on the average newspaper of the country.

Even in the national field, the largest part of the daily news coming from all sources these days, has a direct bearing on the war story. As an illustration, of some 25 columns of national news printed in *The New York Times* this morning, more than half of that amount came from our Washington bureau and fully eighty per cent of that Washington report bore directly upon the war.

This shift in normal news interest has been only natural, because, in newspaper parlance, the "big story" has been over there—it has been over there wherever American men are fighting, wherever American interests are developing. And even in our more strictly national life all efforts have been headed toward the immediate objective of winning the war and getting the men back home.

We have reached the point now, however, where many of us feel that we can indulge the hope that the war will soon be over. We look forward expectantly to that day when men and nations may settle down in peace again, to face the arduous task of rebuilding a world ravaged by conflict. When that time comes, we know that there will be a resurgence of interest in affairs here at home. That interest will be accentuated, I am sure, all the more because of the increased attention the whole world will then be giving to developments of trends in the United States even as those trends begin to take form in the offices and the factories, on the streets and on the farms out in the grass roots of America.

It is because I believe that the United States as a unit, with all its people and problems and its new potentialities as a new world power, will develop into one of the greatest stories the newspapers have ever had a chance to tell, that I'm particularly pleased to have the opportunity to talk to you for a little while this afternoon about national correspondence and most especially about the functions and methods of the roving national reporter.

In the course of these remarks, I must necessarily refer often to *The New York Times*. In the first place, it was as a roving national reporter of *The Times* that I had the experience which qualifies me to make whatever small contribution I may be able to make in these discussions. Secondly, I am more familiar with *The Times,* its methods and its purposes than I am with those of any other paper, and finally, I expect to be concerned with the plans *The Times* may evolve in the future for covering this big story of America.

The coverage of national news constitutes one of the truly great chapters in the progress of journalism and newspaper publishing generally in the United States.

The press associations which have been built up in this hemisphere, notably the Associated Press, the United Press and the International News Service, were formed primarily for the gathering and dissemination of news here in the country. Many individual newspaper bureaus in Washington, of which *The New York Times* bureau, under the directorship of Mr. Krock, is the largest, were established for the purpose of further facilitating coverage for newspaper readers of the national picture as seen or reflected at the capital. Approximately three hundred individual newspapers today maintain full-time news bureaus in Washington. In addition, many newspapers either individually or in combination with others, have expanded their own special news coverage to a national scale. So you can see that the emphasis on national news, as I am placing it now, is not by any means new. National news coverage by newspapers has been a process of constant growth in response to the recognized requirements of the readers themselves.

However, I believe we will soon arrive at the point, especially with the coming of peace, where the daily publications in the United States, will find it necessary to amend and extend their coverage in order to present more properly the events that are going on immediately about them, especially to mirror these events in terms of what they mean broadly in our national life and in the newly expanded international life which this country is destined to live henceforth.

Spot news, as we call the reports of day to day newsworthy events, will continue to be the chief product of the daily newspaper. But as I view the case, it will not be enough in the future merely to chronicle a flood in the Mississippi Valley, or a strike in San Francisco, or a debate in Congress, or a race riot in Detroit or a convention in Chicago. For in addition to the spot story, which any one of these events would justify, the reader will want to know more about the forces which make up the "whys" of the story.

I remember that in our discussions at *The Times* of this matter of future coverage of the national scene, Mr. Sulzberger, our publisher, has often remarked that editors and publishers will find it increasingly necessary in the future to pay more and more attention to the "inside" of the newspaper. What he meant was that while "spot" news will continue to be the first concern, newspapers will find it of mounting importance to develop and explain the underlying trends and influences inherent in the events that contribute to spot news.

Speaking not so much *for* as *of The New York Times,* I should like to say that this is no new concept for this particular paper. For many years now *The New York Times* has consistently expanded its coverage of the United States as a nation in the manner I have just suggested. You have been told by previous speakers of the use we make of press associations in general and they are, of course, of particular service in covering the nation. But *The New York Times* has its own services for national coverage as well. In addition to the Washington bureau, which Mr. Krock has just described to you, *The Times* maintains news gathering agencies with full-time staffs in Albany, Philadelphia, Boston, San Francisco, Atlanta and Chicago. It also has more than 400 part-time correspondents on call, whom we call "stringers," and they send in items from their respective local communities from time to time on a space-rate payment basis. Most of the time these stories are ordered by the New York office. In addition to these, we have so-called "watch tower" correspondents in strategic points in every major geographical division of the country who send in weekly resumés of events and trends for publication in the Sunday paper.

Now supplementing this system, and as a vital part of it, *The Times* has made it a practice for many years to dispatch special correspondents from its local or Washington staffs to cover certain outstanding events which might, from time to time, be considered of national importance. Some of these stories we cover on what might be called a topical basis as, for instance, those particularly related to labor, science, aviation, veterans affairs and post-war plans for reconversion. Permit me to emphasize in passing that in the type of coverage I am attempting to describe, we approach the story from a national viewpoint. We try to forget, as far as possible, that we are publishing in New York. We do not look for, or emphasize, strictly New York angles at the expense of the national aspects of the story.

In furtherance of this kind of coverage, *The New York Times*, about two years ago, created the position of national news correspondent. It was to be his duty in a general way to help to pull this coverage together in the field and to be avail-

able to go hither and yonder, wherever the presence or promise of spot news indicated an event of broader national importance. I would hesitate to relate a personal story if I did
not think I could best illustrate what I am talking about by
telling you of one of the first stories to which I was assigned
after becoming a national correspondent of *The New York
Times*. I had been sent out to Columbus, Ohio, in June, 1943,
to cover a governors' conference and was in the process of
fulfilling that more or less spot news assignment when the
race riot broke in Detroit. It was apparent from the start
that the riot was going to be a tremendous story and I was,
frankly, hopefully looking forward to a message from the
office telling me to go to Detroit.

I was sorely disappointed when the message did not come
the first day, however. One came the day after, from Mr.
James, Managing Editor. His instructions were not that I go
to Detroit immediately to cover the spot news of the riot—
I presumed we were getting enough coverage from our local
correspondent there and from the press associations—but that
I proceed there after I finished my work in Columbus to try
to find out more basically what the riot was all about. I left for
Detroit the next night and spent the ensuing week going into
every possible angle involved in that unfortunate affair. As
we went further and further into the situation in Detroit,
Mr. James came to the conclusion that the story there was
not a thing apart. He felt it was symptomatic of conditions
that had more general application in the industrial sections of
the north and border states whose population had been expanded during the war. Along toward the end of my week
in Detroit I received a telephone call from Mr. James, which
turned into a three-way conversation among Mr. James, Mr.
Markel, Sunday Editor, and myself. Out of it came a plan
under which I was to go to ten or twelve other cities to look
into the question of racial tension and report the conditions,
and especially the factors contributing to them, taking each

city as a separate story. I shall not take up your time with details of the series itself, except to say that, wholly aside from any part I had in it, I think it was a real contribution to a better understanding of the racial situation on the part of the readers of *The New York Times*—and I think almost any seasoned reporter could have got the same facts. In estimating the value of the series I need only to quote social and racial leaders who followed the series throughout. I emphasize again that this is not intended as a "plug" for *The Times* or myself, but merely an illustration of a type of national story, and the kind of coverage, that you may expect to see more of, certainly with the return of peace.

Another illustration might not be amiss at this point. You will recall that about a year ago Mr. Wendell Willkie formally opened his second bid for the presidency by entering the Republican primaries in Wisconsin. For a few weeks there was a veritable field day for roving national reporters, as any political contest always is. Mr. Willkie's campaign in Wisconsin was covered very thoroughly by representatives of all the press associations and a large number of newspapers including our own. You will recall also that he was defeated—that he failed to gain the Wisconsin delegation to the national convention at Chicago, and that as a result of this defeat, Mr. Willkie withdrew entirely from the presidential race.

Although the primary in Wisconsin settled the fate of Mr. Willkie's immediate ambitions, it did not by any means answer the major question which it raised and this question revolved around the attitude of the people of this country, particularly in the Mid-west, regarding the proposition, as stressed by Mr. Willkie, that the United States should enter more fully into international collaboration for the settlement of peace and prevention of future wars.

In order to attempt a fuller explanation of the situation in Wisconsin, and, more important, to relate it more broadly to the rest of the country, the Managing Editor sent me into the state after the primary to make further inquiry—sort of a check-up. To make a long story short, we discovered that there was a very definite isolationist sentiment at the core of Mr. Willkie's opposition in Wisconsin—more than his opponent would confess. It was then determined that I should go to a number of other states to see if the same conditions applied generally in the Mid-west. We found that they did apply to some extent, but not always in the same degree. We thought it worthwhile for our readers to have these soundings and so we made them.

If you will bear with me for just one more example, along in September, 1943, the publisher of *The New York Times* heard that there had been a marked slow-down in the production of airplane engines in the Wright Aeronautical plant near Cincinnati, Ohio. He was told that the decline occurred concurrently with an investigation which the then Truman committee had made of the practices at the plant, and further, that production had reached a low point at the time of publication by that committee of its findings, which severely criticized the company. There had been charges and counter-charges among the Army and the Truman committee as to who was to blame. After some consultation between the publisher and the Managing Editor it was decided to send the national reporter to Cincinnati to see what he could find out.

We went there and spent about ten days. One of the first things I had to do was to take a course in the manufacture of plane engines, starting from the very beginning, from the time the material arrives at the plant until the engine is placed in the box car. I had to go through the whole process, taking four days and nights doing so, before I even felt competent to go into what the situation was. It would not contribute much to the purpose of this meeting to go into detail as to what we found, other than to say there was much to be said on each side. My only point in bringing this up is to illustrate more fully the kind of story a national reporter may handle, whether he is specially designated as a national reporter or is sent out from time to time on particular assignment.

Election year is, of course, always open season for the national correspondent. In every presidential campaign the press associations and newspapers send their national writers —we call ourselves "pulse feelers"—to every part of the country; not merely to try to determine in advance how this or that state may be expected to vote—not to get up any form sheet but to learn firsthand and to present to the readers the issues which may influence the national decision.

In the very nature of the work of the national correspondent particularly in political coverage the matter of his contacts is of utmost importance. One could spend his time in endless and aimless search developing endless and aimless facts, none of which would be of much use to his newspaper and its readers, unless he were able to rely on competent sources and be able to have them help him evaluate facts. It would be difficult indeed to tell anyone how he should go about his making these contacts. It is a matter of human associations. A reporter's best contact in one town might be the mayor, in another it might be the minister, and in still another it might be a newspaper editor. Local newspapermen on the scene are the most readily available contacts for a visiting roving reporter. One of the very best and most reliable news sources I know is the operator of a news stand in Baltimore. Another of my contacts, recommended to me by a fellow newspaperman and one whom I found of particular worth, is a real estate man in Fargo, North Dakota. He sits in a little office in a corner, and can tell you about everybody and everything—how he will vote, his dog's name, and everything else about him. A roving reporter must have these essential sources through which he may collect much of his information and with whose advice he may more properly weigh his facts. Otherwise he would be sunk. The most overworked source of all is the taxicab driver, but frankly I believe he is losing his value now because he has become conscious of his rôle and he is seeking to become an expert.

In gathering and evaluating his information, especially on situation stories, a reporter's first obligation to his newspaper and his readers and himself is in my opinion to strive for the very utmost of fairness. Now, I know the arguments on this question of objectivity. I fully realize that there perhaps is no such thing as pure objectivity in cases where human interests and desires and human limitations are involved. Nevertheless, I insist that pure objectivity should be the goal of every newspaperman seeking to get at the facts. It is the intent that counts most of all.

If I may refer back for a second to the race riot in Detroit, one of my professional colleagues reporting the story for another newspaper, showed me a telegram he had received from his office telling him to send a story on the Ku Klux angles involved. From the wording of the message it was very evident that his editor was trying to simplify the story and was proceeding on the assumption that the riot was of Klan origin. The reporter knew, as well as we knew, after a few hours of investigating, that you couldn't charge off the trouble to any single factor. There *was* a Ku Klux angle, but it was by no means the whole story. This reporter felt under obligation, however, to stress that particular angle.

Now for the sake of truth, I must hasten to say that it is a rare case when any reporter receives directions on how to slant or angle a story when he is out in the field. Most of the stories you hear to that effect are not true. This happens to be an outstanding case or I would not cite it to you. By and large, the instruction to a reporter, if any, is the same as given me on that occasion, and mine was simply to double-check every fact.

Let me say, also, that in most of the situation stories of the type I have been describing, a reporter can prove anything he wants to prove. There are usually enough conflicting or controversial facts involved to furnish evidence on any side of any question. In this connection, I am reminded of the story told by our Managing Editor about an old colored woman down South who maintained that there are not only two sides but three sides to every question: "your side, my side and the right side."

If this kind of news gathering is to be of value to newspaper readers and if it is to serve the purpose of telling the real story of America to the world in the American way, through a free and responsible press, I repeat that I see no substitute for objectivity, at least as the goal. The reporter must seek always to avoid being an advocate. But as Mr. Markel told you last week, we find that people are very fond of their biases and a person's definition of objectivity is all too often limited by his own pre-conceived notions.

In striving for the goal of objectivity a reporter will many times become confused. That may often be one of the penalties of searching too deeply for facts. The more one searches for facts in situation stories, the more complex they usually become. That, to my mind, gives no excuse, however, for resorting to biased, or even half-baked simplifications. Rather than yield to that easy way out I would much rather see the reporter react as did the one who was sent out of town to cover a train wreck. After hours of viewing the scene, wading through destruction and debris and seeing something more horrible at every turn, this particular reporter wired his office: "Sorry can send nothing tonight; all is confusion."

CHAPTER FOUR

THE GATHERING OF THE NEWS

I

By Anne O'Hare McCormick

Editorial Correspondent. Mrs. McCormick has been a contributor to The New York Times since 1922. She became a member of the editorial staff in 1936. In 1937, she received the Pulitzer Prize for distinguished foreign correspondence.

WHEN AMBITIOUS WOULD-BE REPORTERS from high schools and colleges come to me for advice on how to break into the newspaper profession (and you have no idea how many people want to break in) the first question they ask is: How do you get to be a foreign correspondent? The foreign correspondent is the "glamour boy" of journalism. The glamour girl is only incidental, for women are few in the foreign field and as a usual thing they are not assigned to the spectacular jobs.

The movies have turned the foreign correspondent into the hero of a thriller, a combination of daredevil, international spy, Richard Harding Davis, and amateur detective who always outwits the professionals. Some correspondents have fed the legend with their adventure books about themselves. And of course it isn't all legend. The foreign correspondent does get around. He does get glimpses, sometimes intimate glimpses, of the great and near-great in foreign capitals—

the faraway politicians who seem more romantic or more sinister than the homegrown variety because they hold forth in places like Downing Street, the Quai d'Orsay, the Kremlin or—when there was one—the Wilhelmstrasse. He does get a front seat at the big shows that make history—wars, revolutions, international conferences, and the great spectacles.

But ordinarily, I assure you, the foreign correspondent's job is an exacting and often dull routine that calls for a great deal of daily reading, interviewing and investigating. After a six months' round which took in the Western war fronts, the countries of liberated Europe and the Near East, the picture I bring home of foreign correspondents under present circumstances is a picture of hard-driven reporters working long hours under maddening professional difficulties and a great deal of personal discomfort.

They are working for a modern press and an insatiable public under pioneer conditions. You can imagine that to do anything in Europe today takes more than double time and abnormal effort. Telephone services are barely functioning in cities as undamaged as Paris and Rome. The normal services of transportation do not exist. Hot water once a week is the rule even in American-run hotels. Heat is an almost forgotten luxury and a running elevator is a miracle.

Consider what it means to cover an ordinary story in these conditions. Suppose you hear of the arrest of a prominent Frenchman, not hitherto suspected of collaborationism, and you wonder what's behind it. Suppose you receive a hint from a reliable source—and I will speak of sources later— that a new crisis is brewing in the Italian government— whether that is news or not, I don't know. Or you comb through the morning papers—only two-page sheets that contain a minimum of news and a maximum of editorial polemic, but they come by the dozen and have to be read— and you come upon an item that has an international angle, say, and raises a question in your mind.

You have to make inquiries. You have to see some one, usually several people. Probably you have to wait half an hour for an open telephone line to ask a question or make an appointment. When you get your man there's the problem of getting to where he is. There are no private taxis and the buses or street cars that begin to operate are few, far between and so crowded that people hang on the roofs. The army PRO, or public relations office, under whose aegis correspondents work in all liberated areas, since all are in the war zone, provides a certain number of cars for the working press, but never enough, and to get one it is necessary to go to the officer in charge of the motor pool and wait until a car, if any, is available. Often you trudge across the city, this winter usually in a cold rain or bitter wind. You are lucky if you are not too late for your appointment, if you are not obliged to climb too many flights of stairs, if you do not have to repeat the performance four or five times before you get the information you want.

You write your story in an unheated office, an unheated hotel room, or on a bench in PRO headquarters, sometimes by the light of a candle or a flashlight, for the inadequate electric current too frequently peters out. Then the piece has to go through the censors' office, sometimes with a delay for argument—quite often, in fact—and after that the transmission system to New York may be overloaded, or break down, and there's another wait of an hour or hours before the dispatch gets off.

This last hair-whitening blow does not fall as often as it did at first. The worst difficulties are lightening by slow degrees; but it will be a long time before reporters abroad can work under the physical conditions we take for granted in this country. The professional difficulties are a more serious matter. The point I wish to emphasize is that there isn't much glamour in spending most of your time and energy in doing things that the subway straphanger achieves without thought.

The foreign correspondent today is a stone-wall batter,

an up-to-the-minute reporter struggling in a slowed-down, broken-down world. I heard General Marshall say the other night that the front-line commander won't listen to excuses if the material he needs for the battle doesn't arrive in time. He cannot consider the straining agony it takes a general to move and allocate supplies to a dozen crying fronts with tonnage that's never enough to meet all the demands. Excuses are no good to the managing editor either, even if he's as experienced in the field and as kind-hearted as our Mr. James. But he knows the difficulties, while the reader will never realize the sweat and tears it cost to make the deadline for that little story that was buried on page six in the morning paper.

I am not speaking of war correspondents and the incomparably greater hardships and dangers of the reporter who lives like a soldier. Mr. Hailey, who is a war correspondent himself, and an adventurous one, will address himself to that phase of the subject. The reporter of the war is in a class by himself. He is describing the day-by-day action of the greatest military drama of all time. This drama happens to be enacted in a foreign setting, and the more you see of what's left of the setting after the action the more you thank God for that. It is an overwhelming event in itself, not the story the foreign correspondent normally covers.

Some of the war reporters have worked abroad and some have not. In visits to the French, German and Italian fronts I spent days with them at the headquarters of the various armies. A few live in tents with the men on the forward line —which is always a moving line—but most are quartered in schools, hotels or office buildings in towns behind the front. In these headquarters, often pretty primitive, are telegraph facilities for cabling dispatches either direct to New York and London or to Paris and Rome for re-transmission. The communications units move forward to extend and link up the connections as the armies advance. This is why we heard the great story of the Remagen bridge almost as soon as it happened and why the radiotelephoto enables us to see the spires of the Dom rising out of the dusty rubble of Cologne a few hours after they were sighted by the first troops entering the city.

The communications lines set up by the army to keep every antenna of the moving monster in touch with every other and with its multiple heads are intricate and amazing. They are a story in themselves, which I wish I could tell. They are like a kind of giant nervous system, so the physical facilities for getting out the news from every sector of the battlefront, though sometimes they break down, were never so complete. Despite censorship, I think we are getting the daily story more in detail, more promptly and more realistically than ever before, partly because of modern facilities, partly because of more intensive coverage on the part of the press, but mostly because of a more intelligent view of the problem, and perhaps a better publicity sense on the part of the divisional commanders. The press headquarters at the front is near the staff headquarters, and reporters are briefed every day by a headquarters officer, from the top general down. A briefing is a military press conference. It explains the day's action, answers questions, outlines the strategy or tactics of an operation, advises the men where they are going the following day, tells them what the censors have been ordered not to let through.

This "preventive" revelation is common, and not always on the military side. A most irritating instance occurred during the visit of Mr. Churchill to Rome, while I was there. As a result of loud and angry protest by the foreign correspondents because they were forbidden to mention a visit which was headlined in the Roman papers, a press conference was called by Mr. Harold MacMillan, who was acting as guide and shield for the Prime Minister in Italy. Mr. MacMillan really told us everything—why Mr. Churchill had come, whom he had seen, the subjects of his conversations, his impressions and opinions of the Italian situation. And at the end of the recital he said blandly: "Gentlemen, I have told you all this to prevent you from sending a word of it."

A day or two later Mr. Churchill himself received the press. For more than an hour he talked about Italy and all the issues of the war with astonishing candor. I think I have never been at a franker press conference. He answered every question put to him. But of course it was all off the record. In parenthesis I might add that while Mr. Churchill gave a press conference in Washington, and this one in Rome, he never does it at home, and that nothing comparable to the President's exchanges with the Washington correspondents exists anywhere in Europe, either for the national or the foreign news men. General de Gaulle received the foreign correspondents once since his return to France. He had to be browbeaten into doing it and did it very well, but to date he has not repeated the experiment.

This brings me back to the foreign correspondent as such. *Times* men like Ray Daniell in London, Harold Callender in Paris, Herbert Matthews in Rome or Cyrus Sulzberger, just arrived in Moscow, and scores of reporters for the press agencies and other newspapers do report the war, sometimes directly when they go to the front, and always indirectly. The whole continent is a battlefield and not a story comes out of it that is not a result or reflection of war. But these correspondents are not attached to the fighting armies. Like a score of others whose dispatches you read every day, their chief assignment is the same as it will be when the fighting stops: to report on the life of the country in which they are stationed. Although in much smaller compass and in less detail, each works as if he were a national reporter in the United States.

Last week Mr. Krock and Mr. Catledge gave you succinct and illuminating accounts of the coverage of national news at home. You will have further light on the great job of reporting from two star reporters, Mr. Reston and Mr. Adams. The same rules, principles and qualifications these experts emphasize apply in the international field. The aim of all reporting, domestic and foreign, is to give a true and balanced picture of an event or of a tendency revealed in a series of happenings and an accumulation of expressed opinions. If the picture can be made vivid at the same time, so that it has depth and living contours instead of lying flat and dead on the page, so to speak, so much the better. The stories the reporters gather from everywhere are pieces of life and the circuit is complete and effective when the reader realizes that the mosaic they form in the newspaper is life itself, and a part of his own life. News is not only just an interesting, dramatic or informative chronicle of the day's happenings. It is the material for decision, the generator of action.

In this respect the task of the correspondent abroad is harder than that of his colleague at home. The overseas reporter has to be more selective, clearer in briefer space, surer of his sources; he has to include more interpretation in his dispatches. At the present time, moreover, he is hampered by war conditions. I don't mean the little physical discomforts that I have described, but the conditions under which he works, the intellectual and moral conditions, and the picture that he sees is so beclouded that it is very difficult to distinguish the passing shadows from the true foreshadings of things to come.

He is further hampered by the fact that everything he writes has to pass the military censorship, which isn't supposed to touch political news, and usually doesn't. But sometimes a particular censor and the correspondent differ on the question of the boundary between these overlapping estates. I have heard a great many more boundary disputes than the one over the Polish boundary. And sometimes a censor is afraid to take responsibility and a live piece of news is held up until it is referred to higher authorities.

An amusing instance of this happened to me in connection with a talk with General Eisenhower. General Marshall's quip a few days ago, that "You are the wise heads and we are the brass hats," is interesting but it does not apply either to General Marshall or General Eisenhower. The supreme commander is an approachable, unpretentious, imperturbably good-tempered man who jokes with the GIs and talks freely in his rare moments of relaxation. He talked freely on this occasion on the understanding that he was not to be quoted.

"There's one thing I want to put in quotation marks," he said, "and I repeat it again and again. I want to send a message to the people back home."

Well, I wasn't so interested in the quotation—you know we are never so much interested in the things people want us to send as the things they don't—but I incorporated the quotation in a column and sent it off that night. There was some discussion about it by the censors but they finally assured me it was going through. The next day I was leaving for the front and I had to stop in at the PRO headquarters, and by accident I learned that the piece had not been sent after all, because it seems the head censor was afraid to pass it without referring it to headquarters. To make a long story short, it took three days for something General Eisenhower wanted sent to get by the Army censors. Finally when it was put on the wire, his words were intact but several paragraphs of my background comment, which was supposed to be uncensorable, were cut out!

Nowadays, too, there is more confusion in news sources than in normal times. News sources, for the European reporter, are roughly of four kinds. The first is official information, meaning that furnished by members of the government. Practically every nation has now equipped itself with a press department, or ministry of information, an appendage as subject to suspicion as the vermiform variety. In democratic countries, however, this agency is willing to put you in touch with critics as well as spokesmen of the administration. Being pressed for time in London last fall and finding people so dispersed by bombing that they are hard to reach, I asked the Ministry of Information to arrange appointments for me with four or five persons outside the coalition and bitterly opposed to most of its policies. I assure you that the Ministry went to the greatest trouble to make sure that I saw these people. When I wanted to say, "Oh, I have seen enough," they would not have it that way; I must see everyone.

The opposition is the second source of news. I have never known any country in which the claims of parties in power could not be checked by the complaints of parties out of power. Even in the dictatorships, there were always underground groups ready and eager to say to foreigners what they were afraid to say to their own friends and associates.

The third source is the local newspapers. To read them carefully is to get a picture of local life, interests, hopes and fears, that even tight controls at the source of news cannot wholly blot out. The poorest papers furnish leads to follow up, suggest the right questions you have to ask—because I think the real object, the real thing that you have to do in Europe, and I suppose in the United States, too, is to know where and how to ask the right questions. Sometimes you don't get the right answers, but you get nowhere unless you know how to ask the right questions.

Fourth and most important are the contacts with individuals in various walks of life who are in a position to know what's going on. Every correspondent builds up these personal sources and relies on them in proportion as they have proved accurate in their knowledge of facts and right in their judgment of moving forces. Behind these key people are people in general. I knew a shrewd old lady in a news kiosk in Paris who knew more in 1940 about the way the war was going in France than Premier Paul Reynaud did. And that often happens.

Then, of course, there are our own diplomatic representatives. These have become an increasingly better source of information as the years go by. We have now, especially in the lower ranks of the foreign service, an enormous and very efficient fact-finding agency, which makes surveys and accumulates a great many facts, and I must say here that I have the utmost respect for it.

In liberated Europe today, speaking of news sources, the old governments are gone; everybody you used to see is gone and there is a different and more violent opposition, so that many of the former sources of information are dried up; but the experienced reporter soon learns to spot in the new crowd on top the informants who know from those who pretend to know, think they know or are trying to palm off their prejudices or desires as facts. There are still the crowds under the top, who don't change much in any country. In the present confusion, when so much of public opinion is silent, inarticulate or apathetic and groups seeking power have no means of knowing their own strength, appraisal of political trends depends a good deal on knowledge of the mind of the people, and that knowledge, of course, is gained by a good deal of digging and long experience.

Foreign news, as I have said, requires more interpretation than domestic news. At home we are part of the context of unfolding events. A piece of news originating in New York, Washington or Battle Creek fits into a familiar setting. The reporter doesn't have to light up the foreground or the background. We don't know enough of our own country, it is true, and Mr. Catledge is right in saying that the United States will be the greatest post-war news story, for its own people and the outside world. But also, it will be so much more tightly tied to the outer world than before that Americans will have to pay closer attention to international developments.

In our own interests, to preserve the peace we have spent so much to win—and none of you who has not been on the war fronts realizes exactly how much we have spent—this requires more knowledge of what foreign news means. This knowledge has to have more than breadth and surface; it has to have depth. I am so grateful to Mr. Markel for giving me the definition of background I have been searching for that I venture to steal it from his lucid talk on the Sunday newspaper and use it over again as applied to foreign correspondence. "It is," he says, "the deeper sense of the news. It places a particular event in the larger flow of events. It is the color, the atmosphere, the human elements that give meaning to a fact." It is not, he adds, opinion; it is not what you feel about an event; it is what you know lies behind it.

This background the foreign correspondent must supply if Americans are to understand Europe or understand any other part of the world. It is going to be a task requiring more judgment and more probing beneath the surface than ever before because it is already evident that groups and leaders, at least in western Europe, will try hard to win through the press American support either for a particular regime, or a particular policy or program in which they are interested. Before the war European politicians were not greatly concerned about American reactions to their domestic policies. I remember how little concerned the Germans were in 1936 and '37 and '38, for any country. They all thought we were out of Europe. They believed our isolationists. Now they are interested; out attitude is vitally important to their political and economic future, and the competition for our favor will be a snare for the reporter who doesn't know the background.

I am interested in background because I belong probably in the background, but certainly among the backgrounders. The editorial page, as has been mentioned several times in these talks, is the space reserved in *The New York Times* for opinion. But besides expressing the views of *The Times*, the editorials are also analyses and interpretations of the main news events of the day. This is also the chief purpose of the signed articles that appear in the fifth column. Mr. Krock turns an X-ray light on developments in and behind the Washington scene. As roving foreign correspondent whose mind continues to rove at home, I attempt to add my far dimmer candle's worth to the illumination of events abroad.

The usefulness of the "rover" is to add the comparative and relative angle to the more intensive survey of the regular correspondent. He can compare conditions in one place with conditions in another and measure the situation this year against the situation last year. But it is the regular correspondents you have to depend on for the continued story in any one country. If the students follow in the class room the day by day or week by week developments thus reported, in France, for example, or Italy or England, they will have a better idea of the current history of these countries than they can get, I believe, from any other source.

In describing the foreign news service in the opening address of this series, Mr. James remarked that *The Times* is proud of it, and it has a right to be, for it is unrivalled by any newspaper in the world in comprehensiveness and, I think, in the calibre of the correspondents. These correspondents are interpreters as well as reporters, and the complexity and confusion of the post-war period, together with American involvement in the baffling problems and reorganizing a disorganized world, will call for more interpretation all the time.

I consider interviews more valuable as background than as news. The roving correspondent, just because he comes and goes, usually has easier or quicker access to the chief actors on any particular stage than the reporter on the spot. Naturally he exploits this advantage, and sometimes he scores a worthwhile beat for his paper on the strength of it. In my own experience, I have had some interviews that had real news value; among them the first interview given by Georges Bidault, De Gaulle's foreign minister, because he was a completely unknown figure in this county and the foreign policy of the new France had not then been disclosed, and in the same room, the last interview with Paul Reynaud when he practically acknowledged weeks before the defeat of France that everything was over. I happened to be talking to Mussolini the night he got word that the Four Power Pact was signed in France, last of the signatories, and that was news. So was another interview, in Rome, the day sanctions were voted against Italy, when a very depressed Duce, talking more to himself than to me, said that he would now have to carry the Ethiopian war to Addis Ababa—as at first, it should be noted in passing, he had no intention of doing. My first and last on-the-record interview with Hitler just after he came to power was not very hot as news, but it was an extraordinary revelation of the man himself.

Unless he gives away something unwittingly or chooses, this method for making an important statement, as Stalin did on two occasions, the head of government is not likely to reveal anything in an interview that he would not say, or worse, has not said, in a public speech. But he does reveal himself, and this is of the utmost importance to the interpretation of the action in which his character, his vanities and ambitions, his personal reactions, are decisive factors.

The same is true of off-the-record talks with the great and near-great or, at least, with the influential. They often hamstring the reporter, but when an insider frankly discusses an important negotiation that is not yet ripe for publication, or honestly paints the background of a development of public interest, this is invaluable background material. In some form the essential information gleaned in this way is always passed on to the public.

The youngsters growing up in our schools have to be brighter than we ever were, and more serious and world-minded, to absorb the flood of information poured out day after day in the press. I think they *are* brighter—more alert, more curious, more mature. The story unrolled before them is so fascinating as a story, so full of human interest and dramatic figures, that if they are once interested in it as a serial they won't be able to lay it down. It's following it, fitting one detail into another, comparing some happening in this country with a happening in that, or some happening last week with one this week, that holds the interest. Reading headlines only, or skimming through one episode in the sequence, accounts for the wide lapses of information and the wrong impressions of the sporadic reader.

I stress interest, because that's the door to knowledge, and somehow we have to open the eyes and minds of the young people of today if they are to be armored for the world they inherit. Information is their shield against mistakes, against dullness, againt tyranny. The more they read and the more facts they absorb, the better able they are to detect falsehood and bias—because you cannot read a lot without knowing when a man slants his story—the better able they are to protect themselves, and their country, from the perils and the punishments of mental isolation. I do not speak thoughtlessly when I say that it depends first on you and us—the schools and the press—to save our children from being lost in a world they do not know.

THE GATHERING OF THE NEWS

II

By Foster Hailey

War Correspondent and Editorial Writer. Mr. Hailey was graduated from the School of Journalism of the University of Missouri after World War I and worked on newspapers in New Orleans, Indianapolis and New York. He joined the staff of The New York Times in 1937 and was one of the first members of The Times staff to cover the war in the Pacific after Pearl Harbor.

CITY EDITORS LONG HAVE HAD a stock answer to the attribute most necessary for a good reporter. It is "a good pair of legs." And not necessarily shapely ones. Although that helped in one case that I know of. At least the male reporters who had to compete with a very lovely woman in a foreign capital felt that she was able to get our Ambassador's ear—or perhaps I should say eye—more often than they. Perhaps it was just professional jeaolusy. I know a lot of women who are first class reporters. Right at the top of the list is our own Mrs. McCormick, of whom we all are inordinately proud (I looked up that adjective, to be sure it was the exact one) and envious, too, I might add.

Legs are only one of the requirements of a good reporter— I don't like the connotations of the word "correspondent"— whether he is operating in a police district in New York, in Europe, in Asia or on a war assignment in the Pacific. The other requirements, and not necessarily in this order or any other order, are an inquiring mind, intellectual integrity, and objectivity.

First, let's take up the problem of legs—the working kind. In the Pacific, and in Asia, rugged constitution always was necessary. You could find transportation and the finest apartments and hotels in Shanghai, Hong Kong, Manila, Tokyo, Peking and the other great cities of the Far East. The journey between cities, even, wasn't too difficult. But back inland —and that was part of the "beat" of the conscientious reporters—you were largely on your own resources. The war, of course, has magnified these difficulties, almost beyond imagination. For many years now, the reporter in the Pacific and in Asia has carried his own luggage, often cooked his own food, driven his own jeep, walked miles in search of the elusive bit of information he needed to round out the whole picture of some event he wanted to report to the people of the United States. Barney Barnett, of Paramount Newsreel, told me of a trip he made over the Owen Stanley Range in New Guinea where, the best day, they made only ten miles. Although my time in the Pacific was spent mostly with the Navy, thinking back over some of my land service out there I wonder sometimes if I didn't walk almost as far as I rode.

Often it wasn't so much the distance that had to be traveled but the trouble in arranging transport. After three years many of the old headaches have been ironed out but in the early days of the war it was largely up to the correspondent to hitchhike to and from where he had to go. Meeting other correspondents for a crying session in Noumea one day, shortly after Admiral Halsey had decreed that correspondents were not to be carried on planes any more, we decided that a more appropriate shoulder patch than the fouled anchor we wore would be one of a clenched fist with the thumb upright. Even before Admiral Halsey issued his no-flight order in the South Pacific, the problem of getting from here to there was pretty terrific. Not that most Army and Navy people in a combat zone didn't want to be cooperative but they had been raised on directives and if they didn't have one they hardly knew what to do. The Marines, thank the Lord, always have had an allergy to paper work and we largely depended on them to get around. To capsule the condition. If you asked the Navy for a ride someplace they'd usually say "no." The Army would say "maybe." The Marines would say, "sure Mac, hop aboard."

And when you got the ride to wherever you wanted to go, what a ride it generally was. Brooks Atkinson told me his liver never would be the same again after a five-day trip he took over the Chinese end of what formerly was called the Burma Road. There isn't any road in the United States with which to compare it, he said. Forty miles is a good day's travel. On a map, and perhaps even in most Americans' minds, the Burma Road, or Stilwell Road as it now is called officially, appears as a broad, smooth highway instead of the creation of the devil that it is. Perhaps the person who coined the phrase about the road to hell being paved with good intentions, had one of Asia's military roads in mind.

Tillman Durdin, *The Times* correspondent in the China-Burma-India theatre, says the worst traveling he has had to do in his seven and a half year's of war reporting in the Far East was the flight over "the hump" from India to China in the transport planes. He has made the trip several times. They would take off from an Indian airfield where it was 120 in the shade and in an hour would be in the Himalayas at 18,000 feet with the temperature below zero outside the plane and not much better inside. Then he'd sit down in China, in sticky heat again. It was impossible, really, to dress for either temperature so Till just sweated it out aground and froze it out aloft and hoped he wouldn't catch pneumonia.

Anyone who hasn't ridden a bucket seat in a transport plane for several thousand miles has something to be thankful for. They are the little metal seats placed along either side of the main cabin, supposedly shaped just right to accommodate the human posterior. I have yet to meet the person that they fit. Certainly they didn't fit me. But if you were tired enough you even could sleep on them. I did, flying back from the Aleutians with Lieut. Gen. Holland M. (Howling Mad) Smith. Having had previous experience with the seats, General Smith has a canvas folding chair put aboard for his use. Squirming around on my assigned bucket I made caustic remarks about privileged brass, but it didn't touch his heart. Finally I became so sleepy I rigged up some parachute packs and stretched out over three of the seats for an hour's nap. When I woke up, General Smith asked me if I would change places with him. "By God, Hailey," he said, "if *The New York Times* can sleep on those seats so can I." And he did. It's difficult to get ahead of the Marines.

The actual physical discomforts of life in a war zone, however, are comparatively minor compared to the greater hazard of disease. In most of Asia and the islands of Oceania malaria, dengue fever and dysentery are as common as a nose cold in New York City. No correspondent that I know who has served in Asia or the Pacific but has had one of the tropical diseases. Sometimes all of them. For several months in the South Pacific, Bob Miller, the capable young United Press reporter who went ashore with the Marines at Tulagi in the Solomons on August 7, 1942, was quite proud of his seeming immunity to the malaria and dysentery that everyone else was getting there. I was with Bob in the Fijis in the spring of 1943 when he finally decided one day that he was sick. He checked in at the Army hospital that was operated by the Johns Hopkins unit. The next morning when I went up to see Bob, I asked the Colonel in charge of the hospital, whose name I have forgotten but who boasted he was the only man who ever got the best of Henry Mencken in an argument—he took his appendix away from him—what they had found. Up to now, he answered, we have discovered that Miller has malaria, yellow jaundice, dysentery and filariasis (or elephantiasis as it is better known). Just to prove that he was pretty tough, Bob came home, recovered a part of his health and shoved off for the European war front where he picked up a bomb fragment at Verdun that has crippled his left arm. I just received word today, incidentally, that Bob's arm is much better and that he is now able to pick up things with it, and perhaps it may be a complete recovery. Bob still looks on the bright side of life, though. When he was through New York last December he told me the seven pints of blood he had received in transfusions apparently had eliminated the malaria germs because he hadn't had a chill or a fever since. Perhaps that is the new cure.

I should like to make it clear, in telling you of the hardships of the correspondents, however, that I am not setting them up as a special class or trying to picture their trials and tribulations as comparing in any way with those undergone by our soldiers, sailors and marines. It's tough enough fighting a war with a notebook and a pencil but it's not as tough as fighting it with a rifle and hand grenades and machine guns. Correspondents share some of the hardships and some of the dangers of the men with whom they travel but not in as full measure or, generally, for as continuous a period. By the very nature of things we had to pull out of the front lines to write our stories and we lived, for the most part, at division headquarters or in the captain's or admiral's quarters aboard ship.

So much for the legs.

Censorship, both of the finished product and at the source, sharply curtails during wartime one of those other attributes of the good reporter, the inquiring mind. After you have met several rebuffs from gold-braided officials from whom you have sought information or had ruthlessly eliminated from your copy facts you have spent much time searching out or, perhaps, have risked your life to get, you often are inclined to say, the hell with it all, and write only what you are told in the communiques or what you are pretty sure will get by. When you reach that stage, it's time to come home.

Unfortunately—and I hate to say this because I don't like to throw rocks at other reporters—there have been some correspondents who were easily discouraged in their fights with the censor and the gold braid and contented themselves with writing pretty stories about generals and admirals and movie heroes who happened to be wearing uniforms. Or they were content to sit around the rear bases and write only what the public relations officer brought around to them.

Fortunately for the American public, or it would not have had as much information as it has had, the majority decided they didn't like censorship of any variety, even the American —especially the American—and have continued to fight it out on every battlefront. And may I explain here my own ideas about censorship. A lot of high military commanders have told me, and it makes sense to me, that the only information really that is worth having is that as to the enemy's strength and disposition of his troops or ships and what he plans to do with them. Too often censorship has been used to cover up mistakes both of tactics and strategy and keep from the American public information as to the seriousness of general situations that, had it been known, might have headed off some of the strikes and general home front complacency of which there has been much complaint. If you are going to fight a war within the framework of a democracy, then you must give the people the information on which to base their decisions.

Conditions have improved greatly since I last was in the Pacific, but there still is room for more improvement. For instance, the Navy, after the first two days released no casualty figures on the Iwo Jima campaign until Secretary Forrestal returned to Washington to announce that our dead in the first ten days totaled 2,050. I don't see how that information can be of much value to the Japanese. I am sure it is not the fault of the Marines. My experience with them was that they always were willing to give us the finest cooperation in gathering information and the utmost latitude in writing it.

But that is wandering somewhat from the point about the inquiring mind that I wanted to make. One of the best examples of the true reporter's art that I know of is the work of Otto Tolischus of *The Times* staff in Germany before the war, and in Tokyo in the months just preceding Pearl Harbor. Otto was not content to limit himself to Berlin news and observations there of Nazi operations. He carefully read the provincial press, over which Herr Goebbels did not keep so tight a censorship rein as he did over the Berlin newspapers. Goebbels apparently was operating on the premise that the correspondents in Berlin would not concern themselves with the small papers from outlying cities. This provincial German press carried many stories about war preparations, about air training accidents, about Nazi party activities and so on. From them Mr. Tolischus was able to glean background and actual facts for stories that illuminated what was going on in Germany far better than did the dispatches of any other correspondent. It led to his banishment from the country and, also, the award to him in 1939 of the Pulitzer Prize for foreign correspondents. I don't always agree with the selections of the Pulitzer newspaper committee but I wholeheartedly agreed with that one. From Tokyo, Mr. Tolischus reiterated in every dispatch the conviction that war between Japan and the United States was inevitable and immediate. I am quite sure that it was to his dispatches the Dutch in the East Indies were referring when they acknowledged that they went on a war alert on November 30, 1941, "on the basis of newspaper dispatches." *The New York Times* is widely quoted in that part of the world through the medium of the Australian Press and the Dutch Aneta Agency, both of which maintain offices in New York in The Times building right behind us here and use *The New York Times* service. No other newspaper, not even the Thunderer of Fleet Street, *The Times* of London, has the prestige in the South Pacific that has *The New York Times*. I spent a short time both in Australia and in New Zealand, and I found in both places that every door opened to me the minute I sent in my card, and I have no illusion that it was because they had ever heard of Foster Hailey; it was the fact that I was there representing *The New York Times*.

The late President Williams of the University of Missouri, when he was Dean of the School of Journalism there, wrote what he called "The Journalists' Creed." One of its tenets was that bribery by one's own pocketbook was as inexcusable as bribery by the pocketbook of another. That also applies to flattery, to which the American newspaperman in a foreign country is continuously subjected. Of course it doesn't apply so much during a war. And certainly it hardly applies in the Pacific. Quite the contrary. At Pearl Harbor it was constantly made plain to us in the early days that the Navy would much rather we all went home. In fact one of Admiral Nimitz's staff told me that one day. I had the satisfaction, several months later, of having the same officer tell me he had changed his mind, that he believed the war correspondents really were serving a good purpose. And he attempted to do what he could to loosen many of the restrictions on our movements and our writing that still prevailed. So there is hope for salvation, even for the hardened sinner.

The one case in which the military used flattery to any extent was in the handling and entertainment of the "big shots" who occasionally and only rarely visited the Pacific in the early days of the war. They would come out armed with a "Dear Nimitz" letter from Secretary Knox or Admiral King and immediately gain entry to the Admiral's closely guarded little office at a time when one of the regularly assigned correspondents couldn't get past his flag secretary. Many of them were wined and dined and flown here and there in Navy staff planes. Several of them returned to the States to write glowing accounts of what was being done in the Pacific and how everything was lovely, even the censorship. One of them who paid us such a visit came back to write a series of stories in the Spring of 1942 in which he made the incredible statement that "the full story of Pearl Harbor has been told." That was written before they had even a single one of the five sunken battleships raised. The one roving correspondent who came back and told the whole truth—or as much as he could—was Hanson Baldwin, whose series of stories on the early phases of the Solomons campaign won him the Pulitzer Prize for 1942. The one discouraging aspect of his visit, however, for me was that he was enabled to write in New York what I could not get past the censor, that the defensive strategy the Navy had adopted after the disgrace of the First Battle of Savo almost cost us the Guadalcanal beachhead and probably did cost us as many ships as if it had adopted right from the start the offensive spirit that Admiral Halsey instilled when he was made South Pacific commander in October, 1942.

The only place where the war correspondents in the Pacific were subjected to any real flattery campaign was by the sugar and pineapple people in Honolulu who gave us cocktail parties and dinners at which was carefully explained to us the necessity of not criticizing what most of us considered the over-lenient policy toward the alien Japanese and Japanese-Americans in the Islands. They do much of the labor on the plantations. The owners didn't want them deported, or even restricted beyond the absolute minimum.

I have not had a great deal of experience with the British, but I know they are adepts at this business of flattering newspapermen of other countries into presenting their side of any international argument. In the early days of the war they arranged grand tours for many American editors. I was talking to one of the more impressionable of these after his return from England. He had been entertained personally by Churchill, Eden, Beaverbrook and other Government leaders. To him, Eden was "Tony," Lord Beaverbrook was "The Beaver" and Churchill was "Winnie" and he only wished his own country had leaders as brilliant as these. I have a great admiration for the British. My own ancestors, on my father's side, came from that "tight little island." But I think, too, often, we are overawed by the English country houses and the romantic aura that hangs over 10 Downing Street and the Prime Minister's country seat of Checquers and the Kipling version of the Empire Builders.

It takes a level-headed reporter to disregard the dinner invitations and the tea parties and the pleasant weekends in English country homes, when he sits down to his typewriter to give his evaluation for American readers of a foreign Government's official actions. To paraphrase Kipling, the foreign correspondent must be the kind of a man who can walk with kings, but keep the common touch. And he must never forget that he is not a special pleader for any cause, except the fundamental ones of decency and honesty and fair dealing, but a reporter of things as they are.

This attribute of intellectual integrity merges into the fourth requirement of which I spoke, that of objectivity, which is perhaps the most difficult of all to attain.

It is even more difficult for a reporter to write dispassionately, or objectively—it's the same thing—about the actions of a man or an organization by whom he has been pushed around than about those who would attempt to influence his writing by flattery. We are not Olympian, the Lord knows, and the natural reaction, I believe, of all of us is to react to insult with anger. Oftentimes, too, it's so easy to justify a story pointing up the faults of someone who has aroused that anger. I have a very definite person in mind, Admiral Halsey.

Of all the Navy admirals, next to Admiral King, he most dislikes newspapermen. He grounded us for many months in the South Pacific with an arbitrary ruling that went beyond all reason. We couldn't even fly from one place to another when there was space available. His attitude, as expressed by one of his aides, was that there were three ways of handling correspondents: first, give them all possible cooperation, in which case military operations might suffer (which they would not have, since there were only a handful of us in the South Pacific at that time); secondly, give us plane accommodations and other facilities when such action did not interfere with operations, in which case some correspondents would be taken care of and the others would be sore; thirdly, don't give them anything.

"We have about decided," said this officer, "that the third alternative is the one we will adopt." And they did.

Two correspondents who had ridden a mule boat from Guadalcanal, living off K rations because there wasn't room for them in the freighter's mess, bulled their way in to see Admiral Halsey to protest. "Gentlemen," he said, coldly, "I am wasting your time in discussing this matter, and you are wasting mine. Good day." And they had stood on Henderson Field and seen planes taking off, to make in a matter of hours the distance it took them eight days to cover, in which there was plenty of room for them to fly. I took an eighteen-day trip in a Norwegian freighter's hold from Suva in the Fijis to San Francisco because of this no-flying order.

Yet, I don't believe there is a single naval commander in the Pacific who has received a better press than the wild bull of the Halsey clan, one of the finest fighting leaders we have on any front. It would have been easy to crucify him. The red tape so snarled South Pacific operations while he was area commander that it is a marvel so much was accomplished. He was completely out of his element ashore and as a strategist. That part of his story was told, but it was subordinated to the other, more creditable side of his record. My friends, that's objectivity.

I believe foreign correspondence has improved immeasurably in the last few years. I believe American readers are getting so much better coverage of this war and of other international activities than any other nation is now or ever has that there is little basis for comparison.

But that doesn't relieve the American reader of all responsibility. He still must be discriminating and apply some intelligence to his perusal of the news. There generally is a clue in a story as to its essential truth, or evidence that it is distorted, if the reader is conscientious enough to look for it. I don't believe there is nearly as much slanting of foreign news as there is of domestic news, especially of political news, with which we all are familiar. But there still are some efforts being made in that direction, especially in presentation, and the reader should consider the background of the controlling interests of the newspaper he reads in evaluating the news he finds there.

Never was it more important that the reader bring a critical intelligence to the reading of his daily newspaper. Our whole world is in a state of flux. Its greatest hope to find the way to that better world we all want for ourselves and for our children and our children's children lies in this country, I believe. Europe and most of Asia are exhausted, physically and mentally, or they will be before this war is over. When peace comes the United States of America will be the greatest single force in the world, for good or for evil. If we can take to the peace table the same unselfishness, the same spirit of cooperation, the same grim determination to make a workable peace as we have in waging a successful war, then perhaps future generations will not speak of our time as the dark ages but as the period of the renaissance, when men of good will established peace on earth. Never did the teachers of America have a greater opportunity than they have today.

You are like most newspaper people, you wouldn't be doing it if money was your first consideration. I believe your students appreciate that. I believe you are doing a good job on the whole. I have done considerable speech-making, or lecturing if you like that word better, in recent months. I spoke a few weeks ago to the student forum of my daughter's school, Bayside High School, Queens. I got from that audience of youngsters, aged 14 to 17, more questions and more intelligent questions than from any other I have addressed. They are eager for information. Fill them up. They read more than the newspaper comics. Help guide them in their reading, help give them the realization that every day's newspaper is contemporary history, that tomorrow, they themselves will be helping make history.

CHAPTER FIVE

THE JOB OF THE REPORTER

I

By James B. Reston

National Correspondent of The New York Times.
Mr. Reston began his newspaper work as a sports
writer in Ohio and in 1934 joined the staff of the
Associated Press in New York. In 1939, he joined
the London Bureau of The New York Times. He
has also served on the Washington Bureau of The
Times. He won the Pulitzer Prize in 1945.

I—The Reporter and the Community

MY ASSIGNMENT HERE, as I conceive it, is to define the function of a reporter, particularly a reporter in the field of national and international affairs.

I think I should begin by trying to define the word "reporter." I have worked most of the last ten years in Europe where the word "reporter" has a special and not very lofty meaning. In that part of the world everybody of any standing in the newspaper business is a "journalist." A reporter over there is a very low fellow indeed, a sort of combination short-hand artist, freelance tipster, gossip-monger and blackmailer. I would like to suggest a different definition.

The duty of the reporter is to give accurate, complete, impartial and timely information about what has happened *or is likely to happen.* The reporter, in my field, at least, is one who reports the news and knows that the news consists of all facts which, in a democracy, the people must have in order to reach correct and sound judgments on the conduct of their public affairs.

I want to try to expand that definition and illustrate it and perhaps in that way, better than any other, I can explain my job, at least as I see it.

The first duty of the reporter, in my judgment, is to understand why special authority was given to the press in the United States and to live up to the responsibilities that flow from that special authority. The first article of the Bill of Rights set the newspapers apart from all other businesses. It said, in effect, that even the Congress should be barred from taking any action to limit the freedom of the press, and this was done because the men who started this country believed that the freedom of the press could not be limited without being lost and should not be limited if the people were to be guaranteed the right to hear all sides of all questions.

I don't want to harp on the subject of the freedom of the press, for more sins are committed in its name than in the name of any other constitutional guarantee, but I do want to emphasize one point and it is this: that the first article of the Bill of Rights was placed there as a pledge of safety to the *people*, and that therefore the primary obligation of the newspaper in general and of the reporter in particular is *to the people*.

That seems to me to be the first obligation of the reporter on national and international affairs. He must know where his primary allegiance lies. He does not owe that primary allegiance to the owner of his newspaper, or to his managing editor, or to his government, or to the sources of his information: he owes it to the people, and if he gives it to any of the others, then he is not, in my judgment, a thoroughly honest reporter, no matter how much information he gathers, or how enterprising he is, or how well he may write. In fact, if he is wrong on this primary obligation to the people, then the more ability he has the further he is likely to drift away from the true function of his job.

I do not want to overstate or over-emphasize the reporter's rôle; much of it is routine, much of it raises no such moral questions as I am suggesting here, but more and more, it seems to me, in this generation of big government, big labor, and big newspapers, it is necessary to keep remembering and redefining this essential relationship between the reporter and the community.

The principle that governs the press, or should govern it, is that the selling of news is a public trust. When the reporter writes a story that affects the interests of the people and the newspaper sells it, they in effect say to the reader: here is the truth to the best of our knowledge; these are the true facts: you can base your judgment on them, in the full knowledge that in this country the judgments of the people determine our actions as a nation.

The same kind of relationship exists between a doctor and his patients. The doctor affects the physical well-being of his patients; the reporter affects the mental well-being of his readers; unlike the doctor, the reporter is neither asked nor permitted to prescribe what his readers need to make them "well." But, like the doctor, he has the opportunity to poison them, and the main difference, it seems to me, is merely that the reporter can poison more of them quicker than the doctor.

The reporter is thus performing a social and public service of the highest possible value. That is why he is protected by the constitution; that is why his freedom in the last analysis must depend on his ability to use it in the public interest. That is why, unlike the reporters of any nation in the world, he has access to the chief of state twice a week and free entry to the offices of the highest officials of the nation. The British, under their parliamentary system, give the same freedom only to their members of parliament. The right of the members of parliament to ask the British prime minister any question and his duty to answer them honestly are carefully protected. Something of the same authority is vouchsafed to the American reporter. It is the central fact in his professional life and in my judgment the first responsibility he must understand and respect.

II—The Reporter and the Government

James Gordon Bennett defined the political reporter as: "half diplomat and half detective." It's hard to improve on that. If he is to perform the highest service to his community, the reporter must have many of the qualities of a diplomat, but at the same time there must be enough of the detective in him to dig out the truth, even though the truth is embarrassing to his government at the time.

There is usually very little difference in this country between the objectives of an enlightened administration and the objectives of an enlightened newspaper. But the means by which each works toward those ends are necessarily different. A government cannot always negotiate in the open. It cannot always work out its policies and problems in the headlines of the world press. When it speaks, it must be prepared to act on what it says. It must consider not only the ideal but the possible. Especially in its relations with other nations, it is frequently seeking compromise solutions to practical problems rather than seeking absolute truth.

The reporter, however, is in a somewhat different position. He cannot ignore the practical political realities which his government faces, but at the same time he is not limited to reporting merely what the government decides to announce, and he is not obligated to suppress information merely because it might be temporarily embarrassing to his government.

The test is not whether publication will be in the interest of the government but whether it is in the interest of the people. Publication of the Hoare-Laval deal to partition Ethiopia was definitely not in the interest of, or to the liking of, either the French or British governments of that day, but the people of those countries decided the disclosure was in their interest and they made clear very quickly that they opposed it.

I do not say that we always reach the right conclusion when we are faced with a decision of this kind. Sometimes in fact, we do not. Early in the war, when the British were close to the edge of the precipice, a German submarine got into Scapa Flow and torpedoed a British battleship. The censorship was fairly tight there at that time—it is a remarkably open and fair censorship now—and we in *The Times* London bureau were rankling under it. Shortly after the Scapa Flow incident, another German submarine got through the anti-submarine defenses of the Firth of Forth and torpedoed a British cruiser lying off Edinburgh. We were denied the right to publish the fact and finally managed to get the information past the censorship by clandestine means. In that case, I am now convinced, we were wrong. I doubt very much whether it was in the public interest to publish that information at that time.

In the political, as distinguished from the military field, however, the reporter has the duty to be on guard against the misuse of power on the part of public officials. It is only human for officials to prefer to conduct their business in secret, especially these days when they are overburdened with problems of the most perplexing nature. It is not always easy to find time to explain policies to the Congress and to the press, and not always easy to explain them when you do find time. But democracy is not only the best and safest system of government for the people; it is also the hardest, particularly on public servants. *We* have an obligation to admit that fact and stop using the word "bureaucrat" as if it were an epithet, but *they* also have the obligation to take the people along with them on public policy and they must be made to face up to that squarely instead of seeking to evade it.

In my judgment, the administration sought to evade that responsibility at the Dumbarton Oaks conference. They sought to evade it by declaring that the conversations there were "merely preliminary and exploratory." They knew that years of work had gone into the draft plans that were submitted by the four great powers there. They boasted of the care with which they had worked on plans which the public had never seen. They knew that as the conference progressed and weeks were spent cabling back and forth between Moscow and Washington on the diction and punctuation of the document, something was being formed that was much more definite and binding than the phrase "preliminary and exploratory" indicated.

Events since then have shown how carefully the four governments at the Dumbarton Oaks conference worked out their policies and how reluctant they are to make any changes. I am not criticizing the draft charter; it is a cynical document for a cynical age, and will therefore work better than the League covenant which was more idealistic but less attuned to its times. What I am criticizing is the technique. The phrase "exploratory and preliminary" gave the impression that the big powers were just putting together a few suggestions which they would be glad to have the other powers not only read and discuss but amend at will. The small powers have been permitted to read and discuss it, but they will not and cannot amend it at will, because at Dumbarton Oaks the big powers, whose support it depends upon, laid down not suggestions but carefully considered policies.

Consequently, in this case, *The New York Times* felt it was in the public interest to disclose these facts, but there are other cases where it is in the public interest to support the government against false charges. During the Mexico City conference, a large and dignified morning newspaper in New York—not *The New York Times*—reported that the American delegation at the Inter-American conference had come there unprepared and had been caught napping by the Colombian delegation's proposal that the American states should enter into a general guarantee against any aggressor in this hemisphere.

As a matter of fact, the proposal had grown out of a conversation last summer between Eduardo Santos, the former President of Colombia, and President Roosevelt, and therefore we felt obligated to report that fact, and further, to report that in general the new State Department "team" had succeeded in attaining most of its ends in its first international test.

The Mexico City conference illustrates the kind of problems a reporter has to deal with in this field. Down there, the United States, which is the most industrialized country in the world, sat down with the representatives of some of the least industrialized countries in the world and attempted to draft an economic charter which all could adopt. It was a brave enterprise. But when it really came down to the question of deciding what to say about tariffs and export subsidies and cartels, our delegates found that they were so limited in their authority and the delegates of the other countries found that they had so many problems that were different from those of the United States, that the last few days of the conference were given over to devising a formula which would evade the central issue rather than solve it. This was done, first, by deciding to discuss it again at the economic conference in Washington in June and, second, by rewriting parts of the charter into the vaguest possible language.

Some officials would say the reporter's function was merely to report the language of the final economic charter and let it go at that. We felt obligated to tell what was in the original charter, how it was watered down, and why. Otherwise, the report on this particular development would have been incomplete and misleading.

The Argentine resolution at that conference presented a little more difficult question. Three days before the end of the conference the United States and other delegations agreed on a formula for dealing with Argentina. She was to be given the opportunity of adhering to the decisions of the conference and to "put herself in position" to adhere to the Declaration by the United Nations. We found out about the agreement on this general formula. We knew that publication of it would give the Argentine government an opportunity to prepare an answer to the official conference resolution when it came out and that publication might therefore minimize the diplomatic effect of the official announcement. Nevertheless, we reported it on the theory that the people are entitled to know when a decision of this importance is taken; and further, on the theory that it is not the newspaper's function to withhold information because of the diplomatic effect publication of it might have.

The reporter in this field must, therefore, be clear about the relationship between his job and his government. Their objectives, I repeat, may be the same, but their obligations and their methods are necessarily different. This was laid down very clearly in a famous controversy between *The Times* of London and the British government nearly a century ago.

In 1851, Louis Napoleon carried out the coup d'etat which made him Emperor of France and without consulting anyone, the British foreign minister, Lord Palmerston, recognized the coup. *The Times* thundered against both him and Napoleon and was promptly criticized by Lord Derby who declared that since the press aspired to share the influence of statesmen, it "must also share in the responsibilities of statesmen."

The Times was then under the editorship of Delane who

instructed Robert Lowe to challenge this doctrine and he did so in two editorials which define the relationship between press and government far better than I ever could. With your permission, I would like to read one or two points from those editorials, for which I am indebted to Mr. Wickham Steeds' book on The Press:

"The first duty of the press," Robert Lowe wrote, "is to obtain the earliest and most correct intelligence of the events of the time, and instantly, by disclosing them, to make them the common property of the nation. The statesman collects his information secretly and by secret means; he keeps back even the current intelligence of the day with ludicrous precautions, until diplomacy is beaten in the race with publicity. The Press lives by disclosures; whatever passes into its keeping becomes a part of the knowledge and the history of our times; it is daily and forever appealing to the enlightened force of public opinion—anticipating if possible the march of events—standing upon the breach between the present and the future, and extending its survey to the horizon of the world.

"The statesman's duty is precisely the reverse. He cautiously guards from the public eye the information by which his actions and opinions are regulated; he reserves his judgment of passing events till the latest moment, and then he records it in obscure or conventional language; he strictly confines himself, if he be wise, to the practical interests of his own country, or to those turning immediately upon it; he hazards no rash surmises as to the future; and he concentrates in his own transactions all that power which the Press seeks to diffuse over the world. . . . For us, with whom publicity and truth are the air and light of existence, there can be no greater disgrace than to recoil from the frank and accurate disclosure of facts as they are. We are bound to tell the truth as we find it, without fear of consequences—to lend no convenient shelter to acts of injustice and oppression, but to consign them at once to the judgment of the world."

III—Some Essentials of a Good Reporter

I have tried to define the relationship between the reporter and the community and the reporter and the government. Now I am asked to tell what makes a good reporter. That's a tough one, for the imponderables in the question are at least equal to the ponderables, but I'll try.

The first thing that is usually said on this subject is that a good reporter must have objectivity. That, of course, is true. It is a wonderful word, objectivity! But so often when people talk about it, they conjure up a picture of a reporter devoid of any convictions about anything: a true cynic, who doesn't care whether the bill passes or not or whether the culprit is hung and who, therefore, being indifferent, does not intrude his opinions into his stories and thereby contrives something called "objectivity."

There is something in this definition. One of the nice things about reporters, however, is that they have at least their share of human sympathy. I haven't known a good one yet who didn't have the ability to get excited about things, and frankly I hope I never do. Therefore, I would suggest another quality first and, at least for the sake of the question hour that is to follow, go back and elaborate my original premise.

I want to argue that the first quality a good reporter must have is conviction about at least one thing: sincere conviction about his obligation to the people to get as near to the truth as possible. If he has that, if he really believes that his first obligation is to the people and that his duty is to report all sides of the particular story he is covering, then I think he will attain that curious quality known as objectivity. In this *positive* belief, I think there is safety for the community. If he has *this* conviction, he can be trusted. There is always the question of human fallibility, and his sympathy might on occasion carry him away, but cynicism is no guarantee of infallibility and in any choice between positive conviction on this one point and negative cynicism on all points, I would take the former.

I would take the man of conviction for another reason. In this business, the reporter who is generally blamed is the one who allows his bias to creep into his dispatches. This is understandable, for in reporting, as in law, the man who commits a positive offense against generally accepted principles of conduct harms the community. But as John Stuart Mill has pointed out in his essay on Liberty, "a person may cause evil to others not only by his actions but by his inaction," and that dictum applies with special force to the reporter.

We commit our share of sins of commission in this business. I would not want to stand here and have to argue that the American press has always justified our special freedom under the Constitution or that the American press has always been objective or honest, which is the same thing. But I'm not at all sure that, day in, day out, we don't commit more sins of omission than commission. The duty of the press is to tell what is going on, to speak out, to tell not only what has been announced, what has happened, but what is to the best of our knowledge about to happen. Nothing is more effective in political life than a fait accompli. Nobody knows this better than the politician. It is therefore the duty of the reporter to get at the facts as quickly as possible, and this, you may be sure, is the hardest and most hazardous job we have.

It is hard and hazardous for many reasons. Officials do not want information to be released until they have polished their texts and marshalled their arguments. This is natural: it gives them a great advantage in the debate that follows. I do not share the fears that there is a Machiavellian plot in Washington to limit the freedom of the press, but some of

our officials do like to "time" their releases to promote acceptance of their policies. I think the administration has the right
to work out its policies without undue interference from the
press; I do not think they have the right to hold up that
decision until they can create the right atmosphere for its
acceptance.

Consequently, I think the reporter has an obligation to dig
out the facts between the day of official decision and the day
of publication, even if he has to withstand the ire of the
officials and his competitors to do so. And to perform this
important job, I would prefer the man who is a little crazy
on the subject of serving the people to the cynic whose
indifference might convince him it wasn't worth the
bother.

The second quality a good reporter in this field must have
is respect for the difficulty of his job and for the complexity
of the issues of his generation. Bill Lewis used to advise
young reporters to take their job, but never themselves,
seriously. That says it better than I could and the only amendment I would make is that it applies to veteran reporters as
much as to young reporters.

The more you dig into the fundamental problems of our
day the more, I think, you must conclude that the essential
conflict is not always between right and wrong, as it is so
often reported, but between right and right. It is an unusually
confident man who can be very dogmatic today in deciding
who is right and who is wrong on such problems as how to
make and keep the peace, how to convert our wartime economy
back to the ways of peacetime living, and how to produce full
employment. The complexity of these problems and the way
they impinge on the lives and future of all our people suggest
that a reporter in Washington these days must study the
major questions of the day harder than any generation of
reporters ever studied before and that he would be wise to
take a little humility along with him in his studies. If he does

that, he is not so likely to write prematurely or to intrude his own opinions into his dispatches.

Finally, of course, a reporter in Washington or in any other capital must prepare himself for his job. A sports reporter who does not know the rules of football cannot give an intelligent account of the game he is assigned to cover. Similarly, a reporter who does not "bone up" on the economic and financial problems of our times cannot very well give an accurate account of the monetary plan devised at Bretton Woods. It is, of course, at this point that your job and ours coincides. There probably has never been a time in history when the reporter has had such an obligation to report what Lester Markel has defined as "the deeper sense of the news." And this of course means that if the reporter is to relate the events of the day to the *causes* of those events, which lie in the past, and to the *implications* of those events, which lie in the future, he necessarily must not only educate himself well but keep on educating himself as he goes along.

In the last analysis, the reporter cannot take away from any assignment much more than he brings to it. If he brings to his job in Washington a sound knowledge of the history of his country and its relation to the world, if he brings to it an understanding of the complex issues of his generation, and if he prepares for his assignment with the same industry as the men who are interested in persuading him that their particular side of the story is best, then he is likely to report on it with some degree of accuracy and understanding. If he does not, then his reporting is naturally limited and he is open to the subjective arguments of every plausible advocate on every side.

There are, of course, dozens of other qualities a reporter should have: enterprise, industry, sincerity. But I am convinced that if he has these three: (1) a sense of responsibility about his obligation to the people, (2) a sense of the complexity of the issues of the day, and (3) a good and growing fund of information especially about the history and economics of his country, then many of the other necessary qualities of a good reporter are likely to follow. The well educated reporter who has conviction about his obligation to the community is likely to be enterprising, industrious and honest in seeking the truth. If he has a healthy respect for the complexity of modern problems, he is not likely to go off carelessly and report only one side of the story. If he has a solid education and realizes that he must keep educating himself, he is likely to see not only today's story but its relation to the past and future. If, on top of this, he has a little humility, he is unlikely to intrude his opinions into his dispatches. In summary, if he has all these things, he will be a pretty good reporter. In fact, with all these qualities, he would be pretty good at almost anything.

IV—THE NEWSPAPER AND THE TEACHER

In closing, let me say a few words about the use of the newspaper in the schools. Some of my colleagues who have talked to you in this series, perhaps out of modesty and perhaps because they help make policy for *The Times*, have talked about newspapers in general and their value as textbooks. I don't think you can generalize about how useful newspapers would be in the classroom any more than you can generalize about books. The question, it seems to me, is *what kind of books*, and *what kind of newspapers*. You would hesitate to teach biased history; you would feel obligated to find, not the perfect historian, because there is no such thing, but the historian who seemed to you to get nearest to the facts. The obligation would seem to me to be precisely the same with regard to the use of newspapers.

There are all kinds of newspapers. Some seek primarily to inform the reader about the most important developments of the day, others seek to entertain him and to inform him incidentally. Some newspapers report the news from one point of view, some from a totally different point of view. Some seek to inform him mainly about particular developments and trends which they sincerely believe to be detrimental to progress, others report the news mainly in accordance with the personal wishes of the owners of the paper. What, therefore, is the situation on *The Times*? As you may have noticed, this is not exactly what you would call a frivolous newspaper. We pride ourselves on the fact that we try to give every reader more about the subject he happens to be particularly interested in, be it the Western Front or the New York Giants, than he can get in any other general daily newspaper in the world. This gives *The Times* a girth which is sometimes a little terrifying. But if you are strong and patient, you can find a remarkable quantity of educational material in it.

The size of *The Times* and its staff is a constant source of humor among our competitors. In Washington, they like to say that every high official starts his press conference by introducing *The New York Times* men to each other. But I want to make a point to you about this. Some newspapers keep one or two reporters in Washington and expect them to sit in the office and send between half a dozen and a dozen stories a day to the newspaper. The next morning when the paper comes out, the casual reader may see these ten so-called "special" stories to the paper and conclude that the newspaper was really giving them "special" coverage. As a matter of fact, the men who wrote the stories probably had so much to do in getting the stories together and sending them from the capital to the newspaper that all they did was to rewrite the official handouts, some of which might have been accurate and complete, and some of which might have been neither.

There is, therefore, a great difference between a newspaper which has what we call a small rewrite battery covering Washington and *The Times*, which has about eighteen reporters there, each concentrating more or less on a given subject. We have an old New York schoolteacher on our staff down there who illustrates the point better than anybody in this business. He is Louis Stark, who won the Pulitzer Prize a year or so ago for his reporting of labor news. Mr. Stark was concentrating on labor news about ten years before most newspapers in this country started assigning men to the field of labor and today he is recognized not only by the labor leaders but by officials of government and industry as one of the outstanding authorities in the United States in this field.

Finally, let me give you a reporter's point of view of his freedom to write the truth on this newspaper. I don't say, with Mr. Duranty, I write as I please. I am not free to intrude my opinions into my dispatches, and in the process of selecting the 125,000 words out of the million Mr. James told you about, what I like to call my dispatches sometimes get lopped off in a pretty drastic fashion.

But Mr. Duranty is essentially if not literally correct. We are constantly tilting with these great men on the Third Floor upstairs, but none of them has ever, on any occasion, instructed me to make the facts conform to their idea of what the facts were, or to change a story in order to make it conform to the editorial policy of *The Times*. If you come to a newspaper forum with suspicions in your mind about newspapers in general doctoring the news columns, I don't blame you. It happens too often in the American press. You can probably find a few cases where somebody on *The Times* wrote a story up or played a story down because he happened to think that that would please somebody or other in the management of this paper. But all I can say to you, in all sincerity, is this: Nobody on this newspaper, to my knowledge, seeks to change the facts in a dispatch in order to make them conform to his or the newspaper's views; nobody tells the reporters to go and get anything but the facts. In other words, there is nothing in the policy of this newspaper that prevents me from putting into practice the principles I out-lined above. My responsibility is to the people; I recognize that, and so does the publisher and so do the editors. That is a great protection not only for reporters but for teachers, and what is more important, for the democratic process whose future lies so much in your hands and ours.

THE JOB OF THE REPORTER

II

By Frank S. Adams

Mr. Adams joined the news staff of The New York Times in 1925 and has had extensive experience in covering news stories in New York and elsewhere throughout the nation.

NOT VERY LONG AGO a new copy boy began working nights in *The Times* news room. He was a brash young man of a type that I am afraid you know too well. On his second night on the job he marched over to the Night Managing Editor and announced that he had been a copy boy long enough; he wanted to be made a reporter. Slightly taken aback, the Night Managing Editor asked him what made him think he was qualified to be a reporter.

"Oh," replied the lad. "I've been waching them. It's easy."

His conclusion was only one of many current notions about reporting which reporters, at least, think are a trifle odd. There are those who, under the influence of "The Front Page" and similar dramas, are quite sure that all reporters are tough, cop-baiting rowdies with a bottle always in one pocket. Then there is the school which has derived its mental picture of reporters from the movies in which the cub reporter trails down the gangsters, rescues the millionaire's beautiful daughter, and dashes into the office shouting "hold the presses!" while he dashes off a front page story about his exploits. And there is the comic strip school, inclined to think of reporters as snoopy youths who prowl around with pencil and notebook, sticking their noses into matters that are none of their business.

To all who hold these beliefs may I say: reporting isn't like that at all. Reporting is the application of curiosity directed by intelligence, and disciplined by standards of accuracy and fairness, to the current happenings of the world. The men and women who practice it for the most part look upon it as a stimulating and socially useful profession, in which they are eager to rise as far as their opportunities and their native abilities permit.

In order to describe their daily work to you, I must necessarily outline the organization into which they fit, the network by which the news of this vast and populous metropolitan area is covered. Most people are vaguely aware, if they stop to think about the matter at all, that it would be impossible for any newspaper to maintain a staff large enough to ensure that a reporer would be at hand when some newsworthy incident happens. But very few of them have any clear idea of the careful organization and planning that are devoted to getting a reporter to the spot where the news is.

Basically, the local news staff of a metropolitan newspaper is organized with the intention of having a qualified reporter assigned to every point or field of activity which originates a considerable volume of news. But because news is so indefinable, and may originate at so many and such unexpected places, the City Editor keeps on hand in the office a staff of general assignment reporters and rewrite men to constitute a mobile reserve for handling the news that doesn't flow through the conventional channels.

You may wonder how reporters get to the scene of a fire or a crime or a major accident in time to find out what happened. All such news is lumped together in newspaper terminology as police news, because we usually find out about it through the police department. In normal times the police department of New York City has nearly 19,000 men watching over it daily. They report hundreds of incidents daily to the telegraph bureau at Police Headquarters, which duly lists each on a slip of paper and makes it available to the reporters assigned there.

Most of these incidents are trivial. "Man slips and breaks his leg in front of 680 Broadway. Removed to Bellevue Hospital." Or "One alarm fire at 16 Orchard Street. Damage slight." But occasionally one gives a clue to a story. It might be "Woman clawed by bear in Central Park Zoo" or "B.M.T. Subway tied up at Canal Street Station." It is the primary function of the Police Headquarters reporters to winnow these from the insignificant ones and to relay them speedily to the day or night city desk.

For the speedy and efficient coverage of such news every newspaper maintains a staff of reporters known as district men, each of whom is responsible for the police news of a specified area. Thus one man covers the Headquarters district, consisting of Manhattan south of Fourteenth Street; another man the West Side, running from Fourteenth Street to 125th Street, and from Fifth Avenue to the North River, and so on all over the city. To complete the network, *The Times* maintains staff men in Jersey City, Newark, Westchester County and Nassau County, who are supplemented by local correspondents in each of the smaller suburban communities.

To give you a step by step account of how a district man covers a story, may I tell you of a story from my own district days years ago, which, however, would be handled in substantially the same way today. And if in illustrating the mechanics of reporting local news, I seem to draw excessively on my own experience, may I explain that I do so solely because this is the source most readily available to me, and not because I claim to have had unique adventures.

I was in the night chief's office in Police Headquarters about 9 o'clock one evening when he was notified there had been a wreck on the Sixth Avenue Elevated near Rector Street. I ran to the street and flagged a taxi—in those days you could get one—and hurried to the scene. On the way I put my police card in my hat, so I would be free to move around within the police lines I knew would be established to hold back the street crowds.

When I got there I saw that firemen had put up extension ladders to the elevated roadway and that policemen and firemen were helping passengers down to the street level. Other firemen were putting out a fire in the wreckage overhead. I immediately began buttonholing as many as possible of the passengers. I knew, of course, that I wouldn't get a very coherent account of what had happened from them in their excitement, but this nevertheless was an essential ingredient of the story, what newspaper men call "eyewitness stuff."

Then, with the district men of the other papers, I talked to the police inspector in charge, to the detectives who had already begun an investigation, to the fire chief who had directed the fighting of the flames; to officials of the district attorney's office, the transit commission, and the medical examiner's office, and finally to the plain, ordinary cops who were compiling the lists of the dead and injured.

In little more than an hour from the time I left Headquarters I began looking for a phone to call my office—no easy matter in that neighborhood at that hour. Luckily I found one in a nearby speakeasy—that's how long ago it was —and gave my story to a crack rewrite man. He batted out a column in time to make the first edition with all of the essential facts about the wreck. The first edition story was amplified, of course, in later editions as additional details came to light.

Please don't let me give you the impression that police news is the most important element in local news. Far from it! For many years now, in the more reputable papers at least, the emphasis has all been on the constructive side of the news: on the doings of government, on social and economic trends, and on conflicts in the arena of ideas as competing groups battle to sway public opinion in their favor. But I find so many intelligent and well-informed people who are curious about the mechanics of covering police news that I have dealt with it in more detail than its relative news value deserves.

The many other strategic points and areas which have to be covered for the news they generate fall into two categories: those centering at a particular office or organization, and those which have no geographical basis, but concern some intangible field of human activity. In the first grouping fall such beats as City Hall, the Supreme Court, the Federal Building, OPA Headquarters, the Criminal Courts Building and the District Attorney's office, the State Office Buildings, and Selective Service Headquarters.

Reporters covering each of these places regularly are expected to familiarize themselves with its history and background, with its legal authority and responsibility, with its normal procedure, and with the chief problems currently before it. In addition they should maintain close and if possible friendly relations with the principal officials with whom they come in daily contact. A friendly judge or commissioner has many times put reporters on the track of a story that would otherwise have been missed.

Some of these places—City Hall, for instance—have been beats ever since this method of covering the news was evolved, and will doubtless continue to be for years to come. Other beats develop to meet a specific situation, flourish for a while, and then disappear. As an example I might cite the way in which the news of the sinkings of merchant ships by German submarines off our East Coast was handled in our first year in the war.

Third Naval District Headquarters in this city released the first news of the torpedoing of an American ship in our own waters in mid-January. I was assigned to cover the story; the City Editor and I both assumed it would be a one-day, spot news assignment. But the next day there was another sinking, and the third day another. Soon survivors began to reach port and were available for interviews. Then the Navy arranged a press conference at which Secretary Knox and other high officials discussed the problem.

Soon the scope of the work was broadened in another way. The Canadian passenger liner Lady Hawkins was sunk in West Indian waters, with the loss of more than 250 lives, including those of many women and children. Fragmentary details of the disaster came into the office from several different West Indian and Bahama ports to which survivors had been taken. A few additional facts were obtained at the line's offices here; still more were released by the Canadian government in Ottawa. Some one had to put all this information into a single coherent, organized story, and so it was turned over to me.

From that day on the handling of submarine sinkings anywhere along our Atlantic Coast was made a regular beat in *The Times* office. It had the advantage, from the editors' standpoint, of preventing a great deal of duplication. By that time the Navy had imposed a ban on the publication of the names of the ships sunk, although it would make the names available in confidence to the man covering the story. And so when a story came in from an unnamed "East Coast port" about the sinking of "a medium-sized tanker," it required someone who was in close daily touch with the situation to recognize whether this was or was not the same medium-sized tanker that had been reported sunk in a dispatch from another East Coast port three days earlier.

I wrote so many thousands of words that Winter and Spring about ships sinking so many miles off our coast and survivors swimming through oil-coated seas to life rafts to which they clung for so many days that it was a source of very great relief to me, not only as a patriot but also as a newspaper man, when the Navy drove the U-boats from our waters and thereby put an end to that particular beat.

Many of the most important beats are those which have a topical rather than a geographical basis. Politics is the oldest and probably the most news-productive of these beats, but there are many others. Labor news, for instance, is a highly specialized field of great importance. Aviation, science, religion, education and art are other beats which are covered by specialists.

The basic principles for covering any of these beats are identical: first acquire as broad and comprehensive a knowledge of the subject matter as possible, and then cultivate the acquaintance, and if possible the friendship, of leading personalities in the field. But the reporters who cover these beats have certain unusual difficulties and temptations to overcome, apart from the usual tribulations of all newspaper men, which deserve some mention.

The most insidious temptation is for a reporter to allow himself to be converted into a personal publicity agent for some influential news source with whom he has frequent contacts. There are high public officials, and other important personages who resort to flattery to gain undue influence with reporters, or who throw their favorites an occasional exclusive story. But the reporter who falls for these devices always discovers that there is a quid pro quo; that he is expected to float trial balloons, which his source can disavow if the public reaction is unfavorable; or that he must give his "friend" something more than a fair break in controversial stories.

Conversely, there are other important people who resort to tactics of intimidation to try to get better than an even break in the news. These are the people who threaten to call up your boss and complain you are being unfair. Plenty of them will make good on their threats, too, but fortunately the higher executives of most self-respecting newspapers have long since learned that the best way to deal with these gentry is to back up their reporters. The cleverer members of the intimidatory school resort to more indirect methods. They toss your rival a good exclusive to make you look bad in the eyes of your City Editor.

The best defense a reporter on a beat can present to either of these forms of attack is to strive to the limit of his ability to develop a reputation for integrity. Of course he must also show the usual qualities of a good reporter in any field—alertness to recognize news, and persistence in digging it up—but to the beat man more than any other a good name for trustworthiness and fairness is an asset of tremendous value.

Perhaps the outstanding exclusive local story in New York newspaper history, in the modern era at least, was the direct reward of rock-like integrity. I refer to the story by Lauren D. Lyman, then aviation editor of *The Times*, of the departure of Colonel Charles A. Lindbergh and his family to a residence in England to get away from the annoyances to which they were being subjected at that time in this country. The story created an international sensation when it was published, exclusively in *The Times*.

Mr. Lyman had had frequent, and often difficult, dealings with Mr. Lindbergh from the time that the latter flew in from the West, an unknown mail pilot who was planning to fly the Atlantic. When Colonel Lindbergh returned, world-famous, from his successful flight to Paris, he developed an acute dislike for all reporters as a result of the tremendous barrage of personal publicity to which he was subjected. He became an extremely difficult person with whom to deal, but Mr. Lyman never allowed that fact to deter him from fair, objective reporting.

Gradually through the ensuing years Colonel Lindbergh learned from his associates in aviation that Mr. Lyman was universally regarded as a man who could be trusted. He himself came to confide many matters which would have made first page beats to Mr. Lyman, and he found that his confidence was never violated. And so when he decided to take his family abroad, and wanted to be sure that the story would be held a secret until they were far out at sea, it was to Mr. Lyman that he confided it. It brought Mr. Lyman the well-deserved reward of the Pulitzer prize for reporting that year.

A reputation for integrity played an important part, although in different fashion, in another big exclusive story by a *Times* man covering a beat. The reporter in this instance was James A. Hagerty, then and now the first string political reporter of *The Times*. In the period between the election of Herbert Hoover to the Presidency and his inauguration, Mr. Hagerty learned that the President-elect had decided to offer the post of Secretary of State in his administration to Henry L. Stimson, then Governor General of the Philippines.

Seldom has any story created quite such a turmoil within a newspaper office as did that one. Washington threw it down as hard as it could. The pundits who were supposed to know the intentions of the incoming administration labeled it "ridiculous" and "preposterous." But Mr. Hagerty stood his ground, and because of its faith in his integrity, *The Times* printed his story. It was greeted with a chorus of denials from all sides, but months later, events bore out Mr. Hagerty's accuracy.

General assignment reporters are the hardest of all to describe and classify, because there are so many different kinds and they do such different work. But I think that they might be said to fall into three large groupings: cubs who are just learning the ropes of the newspaper business; reporters who have shown special talent for handling human interest or humorous or other kinds of feature stories, and experienced, versatile reporters who can be trusted with the most difficult and delicate assignments.

To give you some idea of the scope and variety of the work of a general assignment reporter, may I mention some stories from my own recent experience: the arrival of the diplomatic exchange liner Gripsholm with hundreds of wounded

American war veterans, repatriated from Nazi prison camps; the consecration of a bishop in St. Patrick's Cathedral; the arrest of two Nazi spies by the F.B.I.; a major foreign policy address by Governor Dewey; a Communist rally in Madison Square Garden at which Earl Browder laid down the current party line; a series of stories on the background and need for the proposed drafting of nurses into the armed forces; the disbarment proceedings against former Magistrate Aurelio, and a Conference on Philosophy, Science and Religion at Columbia University.

How does a general assignment reporter go to work on a story? In general, very much the same way you unravel a knot. You seize the handiest strand of the story and tug on it until you either make some headway or decide to abandon it in favor of another. As you straighten out one kink, it leads you to another. Pretty soon, if you are persistent and lucky, you have your story. There are various ways of operating. I have known reporters who practiced all kinds of devious methods, such as cultivating the secretaries of important men, or posing as detectives, or insurance salesmen, or anything but what they actually were. Personally I favor the direct approach. I go to the person who might reasonably be expected to have the information I am after; tell him who I am, and ask him what I want to know. I find that system works pretty well. And I am quite sure that most experienced reporters would agree with me.

Just to avoid giving the impression that we on *The Times* claim a monopoly on good reporting—which is very far from the case—I want to turn to a reporter on another newspaper for an example of a brilliant piece of general assignment work. S. Burton Heath of the *New York World-Telegram* won the Pulitzer prize for domestic reporting in 1939 by a series of stories exposing improper judicial conduct by one of the highest ranking members of the entire Federal judiciary, the presiding judge of the United States Circuit Court of Appeals in this city. His stories resulted in the resignation of that judge from his high office, and his subsequent imprisonment in a Federal penitentiary.

You may wonder how he dug up the facts in the case. Mr. Heath had been suspicious of the judge in question for a long time. At last he found the key to the puzzle in the transcript of testimony which the judge had given at an audit in the Surrogate's Court of the accounts of his business partner, who had died. For six months Mr. Heath ran down the clues provided by that testimony. When he finished, he had incontrovertible evidence that the judge in question had participated in deciding cases involving business concerns in which he himself was financially interested. It took patience, persistence, resourcefulness, a knowledge of legal terminology and of accounting procedure, for Mr. Heath to achieve his purpose. But most of all it took moral courage. For if he had made a mistake anywhere along the line—if he had been wrong—he might have gone to jail for criminal libel, and in any event his own professional career would have been ruined. But he was right, and thereby he performed a public service of great merit.

The rewrite desk is the metropolitan newspaper's last bulwark against disaster. If a story breaks that is outside the bailiwick of the district men and the station men, and that hasn't been assigned to a general reporter because it couldn't be foreseen, a rewrite man is put to work on it in a hurry. His principal tool is the telephone. It is really astonishing what a good rewrite man can dig up over the telephone when he has to.

From the rewrite desk in The Times Building on Forty-third street, I have seen a rewrite man cover a train wreck in Georgia and a shipwreck off Cape Cod. In the one case he persuaded the mayor of the nearest little town to go to the scene and call him back with the details; in the case of the shipwreck he induced the commanding officer of the Coast

Guard Station that was handling the wreck to call him back every half hour all night with the latest news on the progress of the rescue work.

In my own rewrite days I have covered such stories as the entrapment of a group of miners in a Nova Scotian mine; a spectacular kidnapping in Denver, Colo., and an earthquake in Santiago, Chile, by telephone. Of course I didn't get as good or as complete a story as would have been obtained by a reporter on the scene, but I got enough to make a deadline with a story we wouldn't have had otherwise. Perhaps the most spectacular piece of telephone work I have seen, however, was when Harold Denny, now a well-known war correspondent but for long one of the most valued members of *The Times* local staff, covered a revolution in Brazil by telephone and beat every other newspaper and news agency hollow. The same trick couldn't be worked now because a censorship would immediately be clapped on trans-oceanic calls, but at that time the censors weren't awake to the gap in their defenses.

Where do reporters come from? I should say at a rough guess that fully half of them nowadays come from schools of journalism. There used to be an inclination to sneer at journalism schools on the part of newspaper men who had come up the hard way, but it has long since been dissipated by the number of good reporters and good desk men who have come out of those institutions. Probably the next largest group is made up of men who attended liberal arts colleges, but got some practical newspaper experience at the same time either on the college newspaper or by acting as college correspondent for a metropolitan paper.

Two of the finest reporters I know, however, had to go to work to help support their families when they completed grammar school right here in New York City. By dint of hard work, wide reading and exceptional native ability they overcame their lack of formal education, and rose to the front

ranks of the reportorial profession. Both are unusually gifted
—one has a remarkable intuitive understanding of his fellow
men; the other has a brain that works with the speed and precision of a steel trap—but I think that their success is also a
tribute to the soundness of the elementary training they received in the city's school system.

In every big city room there are men who prepared themselves for other fields. We have a couple of Ph.Ds on *The
Times'* local staff. Our City Hall man, who has the unenviable
task of getting along with our mercurial Mayor, is a lawyer
by training. There are those who contend that the assignment really calls for a professional diplomat, but to date our
lawyer has done very well. Our first string political reporter
studied electrical engineering in college; our expert on munici-
pal affairs for a number of years was a chemist. On the other
hand, our science reporter, whose outstanding work in that
field has been recognized by the award of the Pulitzer prize,
majored in philosophy in college.

I don't want to claim that every reporter is a mental giant
or a master of learning. I happened to look over the shoulder
of a very good friend of mine several years ago, and discovered him engaged in a most difficult mathematical calculation.
He had written down on a piece of paper the figure 18. Beneath it he had written the figure 3, and carefully prefixed it
by a minus sign. Then, drawing a line beneath the two figures,
he was able to achieve the correct result of 15. I might add
that he has since made an excellent record as a war correspondent, although I don't know who totaled up his expense
accounts for him.

One point that I want to touch on is the great strides that
women have made in the newspaper business in recent years.
Twenty years ago, when I broke into reporting, they didn't
get much chance on the more conservative papers. The tab-
loids and the sensational sheets had a few, known in the argot
of the tribe as "sob-jerkers" because their principal function

was to write heart-rending pieces about the victims of crimes and tragedies. But women are persistent creatures, and have finally battered down the doors against them. Of course the shortage of manpower because of the war has helped greatly, but the principal reason for their success is that they have proved that they can do consistently good work, without asking any favors because of their sex.

People sometimes ask me about the attitude of reporters toward their rivals from competing newspapers. Well, I can assure you that we don't snap or snarl at one another. As a matter of fact most reporters are very friendly and helpful, surprisingly so, considering that we are in a highly competitive business. Suppose, for instance, that a reporter arrives as a press conference is breaking up. It doesn't matter in the least whether he is an old friend or a complete stranger; it is a matter of course to give him what we call a "fill in" on what he has missed.

In general most experienced reporters are always willing to share with other reporters anything they may have obtained in the course of the ordinary, routine coverage of the obvious news sources. Sometimes this may even be the whole story. I remember, for instance, an occasion when Ray Daniell, now chief of the London Bureau of *The Times*, but then the star man of the local staff, missed train connections en route to a sit-down strike, with the result that through no fault of his own he arrived hours after the other New York reporters. One of them told me about it a few days later.

"I didn't mind turning over to Danny everything that I had spent all day digging up, because he had done as much for me in the past," he said. "But what did burn me up was to have him write three times as good a story out of my stuff as I did myself."

On the other hand, when a reporter through exceptional ingenuity, or resourcefulness, or pertinacity or sheer good luck gets an exclusive angle on a good story, that is a very different matter indeed. He is fully entitled to make the most of it and his competitors expect him to do so. In fact they will congratulate him for it even while they are hoping—and planning—to pay him back in kind.

Newspaper reporting is quite unlike most other kinds of work because of the goldfish-bowl lack of privacy in which it is performed. Every morning your story is there in black and white for all the world to read, including your City Editor, and your fellow reporters and friends. They cannot only read it but they can compare it with the stories of the reporters who had the same assignment for the other newspapers—and believe me, they do! This is more effective in keeping reporters on their toes, I think, than any system of rewards and punishments that could possibly be devised.

How much it means to a reporter to know how his work is regarded by his fellow-newspapermen was brought home to me vividly only recently. By an odd coincidence I got three letters within a short time from friends of mine who formerly worked on the local staff of *The Times,* but who are now war correspondents. All three of them—Hal Denny, with the First Army in Germany; Dick Johnston, with the Ninth Air Force, and Warren Moscow, writing from Pacific Fleet headquarters on the island of Guam, made the same point independently.

Johnston put it most explicitly:

"I live and work in a void, completely ignorant of whether my work has been good, bad or inconsequential, since I've not even seen a *Times* in months. It's odd, you might agree, to write and file and then be forever curious about whether the story ever saw the light of day. It will be a sad day to come home and find my effusions impaled on the cable desk's longest and sharpest spike, but for the present I can delude myself and eagerly flip imaginary pages of *The Times* to find my stuff, lacerated by censors on this end and by copyreaders on that."

We reporters think of ourselves as performing a useful, an essential public service. Without the vast mass of miscellaneous information that we dig up daily life would be quite different for most of you. I wonder how many of you recall how helpless, how blinded most people felt when the strike of the news stand proprietors left the New York City public without newspapers for a few days? But we have a more compelling reason than that for remaining reporters, and that is because we love it. To my mind, the one indispensable qualification for a good reporter is a zest for news. I hope that my remarks this afternoon have given you some comprehension of why reporters retain that zest year after year.

CHAPTER SIX

THE PRESENTATION OF THE NEWS

By Neil MacNeil

Assistant Night Managing Editor. Mr. MacNeil be-gan his newspaper work in Montreal and joined the staff of The New York Times in 1917. He has been Assistant Night Managing Editor since 1930.

IT IS DIFFICULT to understand the problems involved in the presentation of the news without some appreciation of what constitutes news. And this is not easy or simple to explain for many ponderables and imponderables enter into the making of a news story, and news editors disagree among themselves about it. News is such a fleeting, illusive thing that it is difficult to be precise about it. It ebbs and flows and is forever changing. What is news for one news-paper will not be news for another. What is news for one community will not be news for another. What is more, the emphasis of the news is forever changing. It is different today from what it was during the depression, for instance; and it will be different again in the reconstruction era before us.

No one has ever come forth with a satisfactory definition of news; and it is probable that no one ever will. Most news editors have tried at one time or another—often with rather silly results, for each has viewed news in the light of his own work on his own newspaper. Of course every newspaper reader, and certainly the leader of every pressure group, has definite ideas of what news is, but a fair analysis will show that these are limited generally by his own selfish interests. Usually this means that he wants the editors to print what he wants to see in type and to reject everything in conflict with his interests.

In "Without Fear or Favor," my study of the metropolitan newspaper, I defined news as:

"A compilation of facts on current events of interest or importance to the readers of the newspaper printing it."

This may be too general and too vague, but it does stress the major factors in news. News must deal with current events, principally those from one day's issues to the next. It should deal only with facts, and should give these so far as possible up to the hour of going to press. Each news story should be of some interest to, or of some importance to, thousands of the readers of the newspaper printing it. Not every story will concern every reader. In fact few readers can read every story in a modern newspaper.

Many newspaper readers have been confused about news by the facetious definition made by a great editor in a light moment: "If a dog bites a man that is not news; if a man bites a dog that is news." This gives the impression that novelty is the determining factor in all news, which it is not. It does make some stories, usually trivial ones. If a mad dog, for example, bites the President of the United States or any other national or world-famous personage it is news at any time. Yet what newspaper would give space to a story about some unfortunate insane man biting a dog, unless perhaps that dog were the champion of champions. In other words, the dignity of the person involved or the significance of the locale is a determining factor.

The ingredients of news are well-known and easily recognized. Its sources are common enough. Its significance to the community or the nation can be quickly appraised. It has been an effective weapon in war and it is vital to the progress of civilized peoples in peace. In fact our world of today cannot function without quick, accurate and complete news. A news editor can recognize news instantly and determine its value exactly although he might be embarrassed if he tried to explain on what he based his judgment. He knows what makes news for his newspaper and its readers; he must, for otherwise his newspaper cannot survive. There is no law in the United States requiring its citizens to buy newspapers. A newspaper can only live on its service to the public. When it ceases to serve a large segment of the public it passes from the scene and is soon forgotten.

There is no time here to go into all the things that make news, and why they do. These are so extensive and go so deeply into the life we lead and the work we do that they might well be made the occasion for a whole series of lectures. So I shall confine myself to a few of the characteristics of news that determine the presentation of news in a metropolitan newspaper.

First, its readers determine what is news for a newspaper. A newspaper might possibly survive without advertising and without many other features but it cannot survive one day without readers. So its publisher and its editors, must consider its readers first, last and all the time. They must gather the news-facts that they feel will interest their readers and present them intelligently and attractively so they will read them. Thus *The New York Times* is printed for its readers and not for the readers of the *Daily Worker*. The *Herald Tribune* is printed for its readers and not for those of the *Mirror*. The *Baltimore Sun* is printed for its readers and not for those of the *Chicago Tribune*. The news that each newspaper prints each day must cover most of the happenings of concern to its readers. If its budget of news ignores matters of interest or importance to its readers they will switch to another newspaper that gives these news-facts.

Second, the news should be objective. This point has been stressed by several other speakers before me, but I think it is important to deal with again here, since it enters into the editing. This means that the news should be reported and edited on the basis of its facts and of its importance apart from the views and interests of the reporters and the editors dealing with it and of the newspaper publishing it and of the community of readers supporting the newspaper and its staff. It means seeking the truth as a thing in itself, a thing that stands by itself regardless of what you may think of it or of how it may affect you. It means that news-facts have an existence of their own and in themselves. This ideal is what the philosophers might call absolute truth.

Objective news coverage is never easy to achieve; in fact it is the newspaper's most difficult goal. It takes years of training and effort to see and record news apart from your own interests and prejudices. Every editor and reporter has his own individual racial, religious, social, economic and educational background. This goes with him at all times like his shadow, and tends to intrude when he needs and desires it least. Yet he must submerge it; all good reporters and editors do. It must be replaced by a high sense of responsibility to his readers and to the community.

Third, major news seldom comes complete and final. Many important stories continue to flow from one edition to another, and may go on for weeks, for months and for years. The story of the battle with the fate of the world at stake will not end in a conveniently-timed victory so that the editor can get it into his newspaper. The bill going through Congress must be dealt with daily for weeks. The murder will not solve itself for the next edition. So the newspaper staff must cover much news that is still in the making and where the facts are incomplete and difficult to determine. Then, of course, many men making news are more intent on obscuring the facts or in coloring them than in making them available to reporters and correspondents. Finally there are problems of censorship, propaganda, transmission, decency, distortion and libel that may delay the flow of the news or make it impossible to print the full truth.

Fourth, editions cannot wait on the news. The edition must go to press on the minute, for it is timed to catch trains, trucks and airplanes. The reader who does not get his newspaper on time because it missed the delivery truck or the train can be quite indignant; so indignant that he may switch to another newspaper that makes its deliveries on time. The result is that speed enters into the gathering, the writing, the editing and the display of many news stories. The story that makes the edition is always better than the story that misses the edition. News often breaks on top of editions, or between editions, and gives news reporters and editors little time for deliberation. This is a frequent occurrence these war days. The news editor must think fast; and he must be right the first time. The method of handling a news story that will get that story into the edition is thus the best method. Readers and critics may suggest other methods, but they are worthless to the time-pressed editor.

Fifth, all news is relative. There is always an abundance of news and never does the editor have to resort to the faking of news to fill his edition. On the contrary his great problem, especially in these days of war and newsprint rationing, is to find space for all the news he feels should be in each edition. But this does not mean that news maintains an even flow; for it never does. One story can be more interesting or more important than another. Several major stories can break for the same edition, and often do. On other days the volume of news may be as great or greater but the best stories will be of less significance or interest. On still other days one major news story may dominate the news and make all other news seem trivial. The sudden and dramatic ending of the war would be such a story. Thus a news story might find itself dignifying the front page one day that would not have a chance of such display on another. With big news breaking even important news stories must be reduced in space and displayed inside. This is especially true in wartime with critical battles being fought on many fronts. Big news usually determines its own display.

Objectivity is as necessary in news display as it is in news writing and news editing.

Now let us consider how the news is written, edited and displayed and made into a finished newspaper. There is no better way of doing this that I know than to take a look at the news staff functioning as a unit. So let us visit the news room of *The New York Times* at eight o'clock any evening— that is, two hours and forty minutes before the deadline for the first edition. Similar conditions will prevail on other newspapers before their first editions. The staff is busy recording the events of the day that has ended in Europe and is ending in the Americas or the new day that is unfolding in the Orient, for the viewpoint is world-wide. All news departments are on the job; the work is fast, tense and almost silent.

Before we go on let me say a few words about a newspaper staff. A newspaper is made by its staff and not by its machines. It is no better and no worse than its staff. Its character and its service are determined by the intelligence, the ingenuity, the integrity, and the courage of its publishers, its editors and its reporters and correspondents. Every great newspaper must have a plant that has made modern invention serve its purpose, but this plant is only a tool in the hands of its staff. One plant is much like another, and the staff that produces *The New York Times* could produce it with the plant of the *Herald Tribune* and vice versa, with, of course, the exchange of a few fonts of type. The staff stamps its character on every page of a newspaper, like a hallmark.

Now let us return to the news room of *The Times*. For

hours news stories and news pictures have been pouring into the office by wireless, by telegraph, by telephone, and by airplane. Correspondents on European battlefronts and in European and Near Eastern capitals are finishing their day's work. Others in China, Burma, the Philippines, and Guam, being a day ahead, are checking on the dispatches sent the night before and are sending new leads, inserts or new stories to cover fresh developments. The Washington bureau is still at work on the activities of the Federal government. The Albany staff is doing the same for the State government. City Hall reporters are at their typewriters. The Wall Street staff has done its job and departed, leaving one man on watch. The sports staff is finishing its account of the day's events, and has men covering all of the night's sports. The critics are going to the theatres, the opera, the concert, the movies or whatever may be doing in their respective fields. Dozens of general news reporters are writing their stories or taking stories by telephone from district men. Local correspondents in dozens of cities have been in touch with the news editors and are sending in their stories on order. News agencies and picture agencies are delivering thousands of words and scores of photographs from all over the globe. More than a million words will have reached the news room before the night is done and the staff has received "good night."

The news editors are also on the job—very much so—reading and appraising and selecting the news for the coming edition. Others are selecting pictures to illustrate the news, or directing the making of maps. From this mass of material the editors must produce a budget of news that will cover most, if not all, of the events of the day of interest or importance to their readers. The stories they print must be intelligible to the average reader. Complex problems in the news must be clarified. Obscure places must be located and explained. Background must be supplied to bring out the significance of the news. Wide knowledge of the news and quick decision are demanded on most news stories. Moreover the news must fit the space available for it in the coming edition.

An hour or so before our visit the assistant night managing editor in charge has laid out the edition—that is he has made the final decision on the total amount of space available for the news and for advertising, and has informed the editor of each news classification the space he may have. He has done so after a survey of the news of the day and consultation with each major editor on space requirements. Besides space for advertising he must allow space for the editorial page, for financial and business news, for the city staff, for Washington and national news, for the war and foreign news, for sports, for society, for obituaries, for amusements, for food and home news, for art and book news, for radio programs, for pictures and for features. In normal times *The New York Times* averaged from 200 to 220 columns of news space nightly, but with war-rationing of newsprint it now averages from 150 to 160 columns—and this at a time when the demands on its space are the greatest in history. This has made the work of the news editors still more difficult, for they handle a greater volume of major news in less space. As conditions are now the news editors can only use about 125,-000 words of the 1,000,000 that have flooded the news room during the day.

News cannot be thrown helter-skelter into a newspaper. This flood of news we have been watching is distributed to the various news desks, each story going to the proper editor to deal with it. Methods differ on different newspapers. On *The Times* we have six news desks: the cable desk, which handles all foreign news and domestic news that concerns foreign affairs; the telegraph desk, which deals with Washington, Albany and other domestic news; the city desk which gathers and edits all news of the city and suburbs; the sports desk which takes care of all sports news; the financial desk which is responsible for all financial and business news, and finally the "obit" desk, which cares for all obituaries, society, the theatre, the movies, music, art, night clubs and allied fields. The editor of each news classification may have as many as fourteen assistants or sub-editors, known as copy-readers, working with him, and often each of these copy-readers is a specialist in one or two sub-divisions of his news classification.

So the modern metropolitan newspaper has specialization both in the reporting of the news and in the editing of it. The copyreader dealing with news from China must be an authority on the Orient. He must know its history, its current problems, economic, military and political. He must know the background of the men who make the news. The same is true with the sub-editor dealing with the news story from Washington, the City Hall, Wall Street, or the Metropolitan Opera. The man who writes the story must know what it is all about and the editor must also be able to deal with it intelligently and informatively. Each news editor must have wide information, long experience and sound judgment in his own news specialty. This gives him the accuracy and speed that the modern newspaper requires. This enables him to select and display the news of the day in his field of interest or importance to his readers.

The copyreader works under the direction of the head of the copy desk, who usually determines the display of all but the most important stories in his particular field. The latter are determined by the managing editors. Each story that is being prepared for the edition must be checked and verified and "cut" to the space allowed for it in the desk's allotment of news space. It may be necessary to have a map or diagram go along with it to clarify it or there may be a good picture to illustrate and amplify it. Or it may be necessary to append some explanatory information, usually under a dash to indicate that it is written in the office. This latter is known as a "shirt-tail."

When the story is complete the copyreader writes headlines for it, the kind of "head" that its display demands. The completed story then goes to the composing room to be put into type and to be placed in the edition. Shortly afterwards the editor has it in proof and he can check on it once more and resolve all doubts before it appears on the streets or goes into the mails in the finished newspaper.

No newspaper is better than its copy desks. Competent copy desks will produce a good newspaper, with all the news checked and verified and properly displayed on the basis of its significance and importance. Incompetent copy desks will produce a poor newspaper no matter how capable its reporters and correspondents. For the copyreader is the guardian of the news and has final responsibility for most news stories appearing in the newspaper.

Copyreading is both an art and a science; both critical and creative. The copyreader must have a fine feeling for the drama and color of the news and a high sense of public responsibility. He must have the background of information and the experience and judgment against which to measure the value of the news story, so he may emphasize the important, eliminate the trivial, and provide adequate coverage. Above all he must know the meaning of words, so that each does the job required of it and an understanding of the newspaper's mechanics and capacity, including its type style and dress. Finally he must be master of the art of headline writing, one of the most difficult of the arts, and the least acclaimed and appreciated, even in newspaper offices.

The modern newspaper headline serves three purposes. It commands the reader's attention; it tells the story; and it dresses the news page. As no reader, or few, has the time to read all the news in the modern metropolitan newspaper the headline must give him an accurate picture of what the story under it is about, so he may choose to read it or pass on to the next story. This enables the reader to select the stories he wants to read. With their space limitations, headlines are naturally restricted in what they can tell. Yet the headlines should tell the story accurately and fairly completely. They should reflect the spirit of the story. It would not do, for example, to have facetious headlines for a deadly serious story. The headlines should do justice to all sides concerned in the story. They should have punch, color, drama, and interest. They must have clarity, and they must fit their space to the fraction of a letter. They should have symmetry. They should be written in simple language that reads smoothly. If you think this is easy, try it sometime.

While the different news desks have been gathering and editing this mass of news and preparing the news of the day from it, the Night Managing Editor and the assistant night managing editors have been busy appraising the whole news picture. One has been going through the original, unedited news copy and the others have been reading and checking on the proofs of the news already in type. The night managing editors must be able to visualize the finished newspaper, for they must give it final form and direction. They have been in consultation with the executive editors of the various news desks on problems of space, interpretation, display of stories, and on the stories available for page one. The executive editors of the news desks have also given the managing editors summaries of the major news stories, so they can get a quick glance at all the news. When the managing editors have sized up the news, they lay out page one, the second front, and approve the layout of other important news pages by editors of the different news classifications. I think I should stop here and explain what I mean by "second front." It is not what Stalin meant. Papers like *The New York Times* are printed in two sections. Page one is the front page, and the front page of the second section is the second front.

The best news judgment of the newspaper's staff will be concentrated on the make-up of page one. On it will be displayed the news that the editors think most significant and important to its readers. This display will be determined by the character of the news itself. When the news is sensational, as it is going to be tonight, the treatment will be dramatic with page-wide headlines, big type, maps or pictures, and perhaps half or more of the entire page devoted to angles of the one overwhelming story. This is common in these days of war with the fate of the world being decided on many battlefields and with many uncertainties and dramatic changes at home. In normal times with an average flow of quiet news the display will be more conservative, and in fact may be confined to one-column headlines. The responsible editors of a responsible newspaper never attempt to make the news more sensational than it is by typographical fireworks. They have the news written for what it is and display it on the basis of its news value.

The front page of the average newspaper has eight columns and the average display layout allows about twelve stories to go onto the page. Naturally the rest of the news must go elsewhere in the newspaper. Usually there is stiff competition for page one display. In other words there are more stories available that could stand page one display than there is space for them. What is more, the editors of the various news classifications will argue for page one display for their favorite stories, and often are disappointed, if not indignant, over the final decision. Rare is the layout that can satisfy every one concerned, and certainly not millions of readers.

On the other hand, as I have explained, the flow of news is never even, with the result that the quality of news for page one is never the same. So a story may find itself decorating page one one day that would be inside on another. Then again editors want to have a variety of news on page one—they want to give a show to foreign, Washington and city news, to war news, politics, science, with once in a while a human interest story. They also tend to favor the stories of their own staff writers, especially if these happen to be exclusive, or to include angles or features that are exclusive.

Great care is also taken with the make-up of other news pages, so that they may be attractive typographically and interesting to read. With the war dominating page one these days much of the city and domestic news may be displayed on the second front. On *The Times,* news editors, usually the editors of the news classification, will make layouts for the editorial page, the food page, the society page, the book page, the amusement pages, the obituary page, the financial front, and the sports pages. The remaining pages will be dressed by the make-up editors—the editors who direct the placing of the type into the page forms in the composing room. These latter editors are limited by time, by news classifications, and by the space available to them; but they usually do a good job considering the rush of type in the final hour or so.

On *The Times* all page layouts should be available to the make-up editors and to the editors of the news classifications by nine o'clock, one hour and forty minutes before the first edition goes to press.

With our edition taking final form, the whole news staff concentrates on getting it to press on time. Every editor and each desk knows what must be done. All stories for the edition are heading toward the composing room to be put into type. Early stories that are complete in themselves are set in type hours before the edition. Others are being sent up with "adds" or "inserts" to come later covering late developments. Late-breaking stories are sent up in "takes," that is a paragraph or two at a time, as they come over wires or are written, with the headlines to follow, so that by the time each story is completed in the news room about half of it is already in type, in the composing room, perhaps in the page form.

The picture editors are checking on pictures and maps in the photo-engraving department and the art department to make certain that they will be ready in time, and are writing captions for them.

The managing editors are at work on their proofs, checking on the editing of the stories, the fairness and adequacy of the presentation of the facts, the clarity of the writing, the explanatory background, and the competence and symmetry of the headlines. Occasionally they will question the accuracy of a story, demand that a feature of it be amplified or clarified, and sometimes they may require a headline rewritten to bring out some angle of the news or to make it clearer. Sometimes the headlines "break," that is they do not fit the space, and these they will rewrite. Once in a while they will "kill" a story as trivial, or old, or order a story cut in length or amplified as they may consider it worth more or less than did the editor of its news classification.

Then again an important new story may "break" suddenly and they will have to shift layouts and arrange to get it into the edition. On still other occasions such a story can be so important that it will alter the whole news picture of the day and will upset the whole edition and they will be forced to do much of their work over again. Layouts should be flexible, and editors must be able to think fast and to act fast.

About half an hour before edition time one or two of the assistant night managing editors will go to the composing room to direct the closing of the edition, leaving the Night Managing Editor on watch in the news room to take care of last minute news developments. Let us shift now to the composing room. On our arrival there the editors check on the progress of the edition to that minute. For the purposes of this talk we are putting a 40-page paper to press. At 10:10 we find that fourteen pages have been locked up and sent to the stereotypers, who are making matrices of them and then molding from these matrices the plates that will be placed on the rotary presses. Among these pages are the editorial page, the financial and business pages, the miscellaneous agate and want-ad pages in the back of the paper, sports pages and some news pages. Twenty-six pages remain, and we must get the news into them and get them away at the rate of about one a minute.

A glance about the large composing room discloses these twenty-six pages, or rather page forms, with large gaping holes in them, some with advertisements in place and the news-type missing, others with news-type placed and space left for the advertising. Still other pages are being held open for stories that are fixed for that exact spot and have not yet been set in type or for late-breaking stories. Type is scattered all over the room, coming hot from 80 type-setting machines. Here is the type of a story without the "head" and there is the "head" 'of another story without the type. Other stories are waiting for "takes" to complete them. Proofs are being "run" to editors and to the proof-room. The make-up editors glance at them and tell the compositors where they are to be placed in the form. The proof-room is rushing through last minute corrections. The seeming confusion may confound the novice, but the expert editors will work with assurance, knowing that everything will fit into its exact space and that the edition will close on the minute. They have planned it that way. It doesn't always work out, though.

Not only must the news be placed in the open page forms but it must also be placed in proper sequence and in proper position and each finished page must be something of a typographical triumph. The type must be placed according to its news classification and in the space alloted to it. Readers are accustomed to turning to definite positions in the edition for the news and it must be there for them. The sports news must go on the sports pages, the obituaries on the obituary page, the review of the latest Broadway show on the amusement pages, and each story must be placed with the map or picture for it, or with collateral news stories. Other news must be grouped by subject. The war news must be placed on adjoining pages with the news stories of each front or area grouped together. Political news, labor news, crime news, science news, social service news must each be classified. News cannot be thrown indiscriminately into an edition, not even the first edition.

It may happen, of course, that an important story may "drop" after the pages for its classification are closed in which event that page may be killed and made over, or the story may be placed elsewhere for one edition. If the latter, it will have its proper place in the next edition.

Page forms are closing with speed and precision. Completed advertisements are rushed to the forms and fit the exact hole left for them, the space that has been purchased by their sponsors. The finished "head" joins up with the type for its story—each has carried an identifying "slug" which makes this possible. The maps and the pictures also fit the precise positions left for them. Everything dovetails into position. The pages are locked up in sequence and rushed to the waiting presses. The minutes are flying with the speed of a robot bomb; but so also are the pages. They must not be bunched in closing, for that would choke the stereotyping department and delay the edition. At 10:30 there are ten pages to go; at 10:35 there are six pages; at 10:40 the last page form has been locked up, and the edition has gone to press on time.

In twenty minutes, or less, it will be selling on the streets or being distributed over the face of the globe by trucks, trains and airplanes.

The staff does not stop there. That was one edition; another is going to press in about an hour and a half, and there is much to do in the interim. All the news editors will turn their attention first to the edition coming off the presses. They will read and re-check every story. Again they may have some done over. A story from a correspondent may have arrived in the office and will replace the agency story in the paper. A good story may have missed the edition and a page may be re-plated on the presses to carry it. Moreover, the news of the world does not halt while editors put their newspapers to press; on the contrary there is a steady flow of it. The next edition must carry all the newest developments.

Before leaving the composing room to return to their desks in the news room, the editors will glance at one particular "stone," a metal table, on which there may be from ten to thirty columns of type. This is the overset, the news that did not get into the edition because it came late or because there was no space left for it. In these days it is usually the latter. This will be their next great problem, for this is news that the editors wanted to get into the paper. They must make space for it, and for all the new stories that came after the deadline.

You will have noticed that every column of every page of the edition that went to press was filled with type or pictures or maps or advertising. In these days of newsprint rationing we cannot increase the size of the paper between editions, nor is it always desirable, so there are only two ways to make space for overset and late news and those are to "kill" some stories, pictures, and maps that are in the edition or to cut the length of many news stories. On *The Times* this is done under the direction of the Night Managing Editor, with the editors of various news classifications cooperating—sometimes. The result is that each story in the edition faces sharp competition from other stories clamoring for publication. As I explained, all news is relative, and the better story gets into the paper. The wordy tsory gets cut, perhaps from a column to a half column. Some may be rewritten. A text may be dropped; a picture may be left out. Some long stories may be killed. These will probably be stories of regional interest, and the edition having gone to their region they may now be left out to make space for a story for the readers of the coming edition.

Each edition, it should be explained here, has a definite territory to cover. The first goes mostly into the mails for nation-wide distribution, while the final is for local New York readers.

The "cutting" of an edition is never easy, and requires sound news judgment. It is difficult to make anywhere from ten to thirty columns of space in a 150-column newspaper without leaving out news items or facts of interest. Yet it must be done, for the mechanics of the profession and the conditions we must face demand it.

I can assure you it is never done because editors love doing it. Yet they are frequently censured for it. A reader gets one edition and later another and finds his favorite story changed—perhaps he may be a press agent or a pressure-group leader—and he can be quite angry about it, and question motives. And of course the matter cut out he argues was exactly what should have been printed. But the editor is not worrying about him; he is worrying about his next edition.

And so it goes through the evening and early morning, until the final edition goes to press and the Night Managing Editor gives "good night" to the staff—usually at 3:50 A.M., although he may keep open until 5 or 6 or 7 A.M. if big news is impending.

Editors do not make the news; they merely record it. They must take news as they find it and print it in the space they have for it. They cannot control the timing of the news story, and the timing may well limit the writing and the editing. For the news story must make the edition. The good story that does not make the edition is worthless. If editors had ample time and unlimited space things might be different; but they have neither. Important news stories have a habit of "breaking" at the most embarrassing times; often at edition time. Besides, editors must contend with censorships, communication problems, libel laws, and human and mechanical failures. No news editor can satisfy the whims of millions of readers. Nor can he satisfy people who are trying to obscure the facts or to color them or pressure groups which consider their propaganda important news and object violently at the other side's getting a fair showing. The conscientious news editor does the best he can in the circumstances, and lets it go at that.

Do news editors make mistakes? Most certainly they do. They make mistakes of fact and they make mistakes of judgment. They are fallible like all other human beings. But they make as few mistakes as they can considering the volatile material they work with and the speed with which they must function. And they try never to make the same mistake twice. They learn from their mistakes. Years of experience teach the news editor to scent trouble and to avoid it. The wonder is not that they do make some mistakes, but that they make so few.

And the responsible editor of the responsible newspaper hastens to correct his mistakes. There is a good reason for this. He prides himself on the accuracy and fairness of his news. He also prides himself on the fact that he is keeping his readers well informed on the events of this troubled world. When he has given them wrong information he knows he is failing in his primary duty. So he gets the true facts and prints them.

Thus a newspaper may be wrong on a news event in one or more issues, but seldom wrong over the years. With continuing stories of progressing events it is not always possible to have the exact facts every day, but sooner or later they become available and when they do the responsible news editor prints them and completes the record. In this light the news editor is writing current history and he wants to keep the record straight. He is anxious, perhaps over-anxious, to keep his readers informed from day to day, and certainly he wants them correctly informed when the record of the flowing event is complete.

When the historian of the future comes to deal with the catastrophic wars of our period he will find the files of the newspapers of our day one of his most fertile and dependable sources of information.

In recent years there has been considerable criticism of the work of the news editors; much of it from the so-called liberal journals of opinion, which, incidentally, give only a biased version of world events and almost never correct the numerous errors of fact in their own publications or give the individuals they attack a chance to make an adequate reply. But I have never seen adverse criticism of the handling of news by the American press by a man or a woman who has ever had the responsibility of putting a metropolitan daily newspaper to bed. Here, as in other things, a little knowledge is a dangerous thing. The person who knows the problems involved, who appreciates the responsibilities that the news editor must accept, is more inclined to sympathy than to censure.

I do not mean to imply that we have not got incompetent editors and venal newspapers. We have had plenty in the past, we have some in the present, and we shall continue to have them in the future. Freedom of the press makes that certain; for we must take the bad with the good. No one newspaper can cover all the news for all the people of the United States; but the press of the United States as a whole does exactly that. There is not an important segment of American opinion that does not find expression in the American press and there is no worthy cause that has not got a journalistic champion. A newspaper may fail in its duty but this does not mean that the American press has failed. By and large the news editors of America and their newspapers do a splendid and courageous job of gathering the news of the world and of presenting it to their readers. They are forever alert and aggressive, and they almost never accept defeat.

If you have any doubt about that look into your own minds.

Are you well-informed on what is happening these days in America and in the sixty-odd other nations that make up the world? Certainly you are; for you are part of the American newspaper reading public, the best-informed on current world events, and American journalists dug out this information for you and will continue to spread such information before you daily. They have supplied, and continue to supply, much of the information that made Americans an intelligent and honorable people and that enabled them to make these United States a great and successful democracy.

America's free press is the best the world has ever known.

CHAPTER SEVEN

THE JOB OF THE SPECIALIST

I

By Hanson Baldwin

*Military Editor of The New York Times. Mr.
Baldwin is a graduate of the United States Naval
Academy at Annapolis. He began his newspaper
work on the Baltimore Sun and joined the staff of
The Times in 1929. He has been Military Editor
since 1942. He won the Pulitzer Prize in 1943.*

PREVIOUS SPEAKERS in this series have given you a
solid repast of facts and figures—well garnished, I believe,
with the color and human interest with which the newspaper
profession is always supposed to be endowed.

You have now come to the dessert, the after-thought, the
coffee—or perhaps I should say "the spinach"—in the form
of the much maligned "specialist," of whom Mr. Atkinson
and I—as you can well see—are horrible living examples.

My father told me when I was very young—"Don't—my
boy—go into the newspaper business."

I did not follow his advice and you can see to what an end
I have come.

I can now pass on to you his admonition with an adden-
dum—"Don't, my friends, try to be a specialist in the newspaper business. If you do, you must have a hard head, a
strong stomach and a capacity for absorbing punishment
which would make even Tony Galento wince."

Seriously—and perhaps perversely—there is, I think, no more challenging profession in the world than that of a newspaperman, and, to me, the most interesting job in that interesting profession is that of a specialist—and, of course, being human, I mean my own particular specialty.

When I say "interesting," I don't mean *glamorous.* Glamour, is of course, where you make it, and there's as much glamour in the composing room as in a night club. But the day of "The Front Page" type of glamour in newspaper offices is about over. The hard-boiled reporter, who reeked of whisky, talked out of the corner of his mouth, and gambled away all his pay in backroom poker games is almost as extinct as the American buffalo. Today newspaper men go home to their wives, buy refrigerators on the installment plan and live eminently respectable lives. (I can hear you say—"How boring.") The reporter of tradition is being replaced—in a real sense—by the specialist.

*   *   *   *   *

Between the newspaper and the school, there are, I think, special ties that make each indispensable to the other, and I would like to itemize some of these "ties that bind" before discussing with you some of the particular jobs of the specialist on a newspaper.

There are two recurring phrases, which give us a clue to one of these common links.

You have all heard the phrase the "cloistered classroom." It is as inaccurate as it is anchronistic. No classroom can be "cloistered" and still fulfill its purpose, which (at least in part) is holding a mirror to life, so that the student may learn about the world we live in. A classroom must be alive—as living as the daily newspaper or the morning bottle of milk.

The other phrase, of equally inaccurate tenor, is "as dead as yesterday's newspaper." But yesterday's newspaper, I maintain, is not dead, if it is a newspaper which has done its job properly. A newspaper's job, like a classroom's job, is to hold a mirror to life. Yesterday's newspaper, if it accurately reflected yesterday's civilization is vibrantly alive. Historians have found it so. Read Dixon Wecter—"When Johnny Comes Marching Home"; read "Reveille in Washington"; read any of scores of books which mirror the age of which the authors wrote. Newspapers are prime source material for the historian, for newspapers mirror the age. Therefore, I say, there is nothing as alive as yesterday's newspaper—if it is a good newspaper.

And this suggests one of the common ties between the newspaper and the school: both try to mirror life; both are vitally interested in history—the newspaper in recording contemporary history, the school in studying and interpreting contemporary and past history. And both—if their mission is to be successful—must speak in vibrant terms and must relate facts to life.

There are other major ties, I think, between the newspaper man—(and particularly the newspaper specialist)—and the school.

First of all, the good all-round newspaper man is a well educated man. He must have—particularly the specialist—a broad knowledge of the world we live in. The school tries to impart such a basic fund of information, but many of us unfortunately—and this is a measure of the gap between our aims and our achievements—do not possess such information.

I am reminded, in this connection of a pertinent story about an American soldier in London. This doughboy was addicted to scrapping; he spent many of his nights off at the "pubs." He was engaged in his usual occupation one night, and spotted a British Tommy. The doughboy sidled up to the Tommy, and said:

"To hell with Montgomery!"

The Tommy blinked, scowled—but then, having read many of the pamphlets on Anglo-American cooperation said:

"Aw, fergit it, chum; let's have another drink!"

The American was taken aback, but not being one to forego drinks, he had one—and again tried to provoke the Tommy. This time the doughboy said:

"To hell with Churchill!"

The Tommy restrained himself with difficulty, but again managed to pass off the insult with a sickly grin, and again invited his tormentor to have another drink.

Now the "pub" closing hour was drawing near, and the American was desperate. He decided to stake everything on one last try. He stuck his face up close to the Tommy's and said:

"To hell with the King!"

The Tommy drew himself up, rolled up his sleeves, and retorted:

"Awright pal; yer asked fer it, and now you're going to git it—To hell with Frank Sinatra!"

Such enormity of ignorance is the enemy against which both schools and newspapers fight. I am sure, however—and I speak from the knowledge conferred upon me by fathering two daughters, one of whom from the wisdom of her eleven years recently told me that I knew nothing about "love an' stuff"—I am sure that the American classroom requires no biography of Frank Sinatra. He is, I should think, the least— or perhaps I should say the most—of your wories.

In addition to the common demand of school and newspaper for knowledge—the school to impart it, the newspaper to use it—there are other ties. The good newspaperman, and the really well educated man must understand—and should be able to form—what Winston Churchill calls "the simple beauty of the English sentence." This is where both of us too often fail—the newspaper in producing polished literary style, the school in training the student to write, if not brilliantly, at least clearly.

Another tie that binds—and don't worry, I am coming to

the specialist—is what I like to call the "habit of doubt." A good newspaperman, and particularly the specialist, must possess a questioning mind, a mind, like that of the man from Missouri, a questioning, inquisitive mind. The really educated man is the man who inquires and analyses for himself, a man who doesn't possess a second-hand mind, borrowing all its thoughts, ideas and conclusions from others. Such a man will not believe everything he reads in the papers—and you shouldn't either. Good newspapers try to be accurate, but being human, they are also fallible. In other words, the good newspaperman and the good newspaper specialist, like the good student, must be a seeker after the truth—which, incidentally can be as "glamorous" a quest, as anything in Ben Hecht's drama—"The Front Page." He must not accept everything in black and white as the bible, everything that people tell him. He must reason for himself and that, too, is one of the functions of the classroom.

There is, therefore, as I have said, much in common between the school and the newspaper.

But it is exactly because both of them have recognized the prodigious nature of the tasks they are called upon to do that specialists in various fields have arisen. With the classroom, this is a relatively old development; nearly all of you are specialists in certain subjects; few of you, indeed, would attempt to teach botany and biology, algebra and Latin, English and history. In newspapers the specialist is a relatively recent development—and one that is still frowned upon by some who recall with nostalgia the "good old days" of the Richard Harding Davis—Frank Ward O'Malley era, the age of the glamour-boy reporter and of the tough guy, the age when every newspaper man was a pundit about all subjects.

But the specialist is in the newspaper to stay, for the simple reason that the field of knowledge of our world is so vast (and much of it is so complicated and technical) that no one man can be expected to keep up even superficially with all of it. Men with specialized fields of knowledge to assess the importance of developments in those fields and to report and interpret the significance of those developments for the benefit primarily of the general public but also for the expert, are now a fundamental part of the modern newspaper.

Specialists, like Topsy, have "jest growed." They have been created as circumstances demanded, to fill a need, a need sometimes expressed by the readers themselves, but in the case of the forward-looking newspapers, in the anticipation of such a public need. *The New York Times* has more than a score of specialists, or specialized departments. They embrace widely different fields of human knowledge.

Some of our specialists are experts on dollars, some on Renoir; some know all of the convolutions of the dance; others the eccentricities of fashion. There are specialists on art; automobiles; aviation; books; business; the dance; the drama—of whom Mr. Atkinson is the great exemplar; education; fashions; financial news; food; garden; motion pictures; music; photography; radio; real estate; religion; science; society; sports, and military news. Collectively, these specialists mirror our world.

The specialized departments of a newspaper are, of course, of varying size and complexity; in the case of *The Times* some of them employ scores of persons. The sports department, for instance, includes on its staff experts on baseball, skiing, football, etc. The financial news reporters have each specialized in a certain field—iron and steel, oil, and so on. The book review has men who keep up with the poetic ouput of the world; others who know the current novels, others who specialize in non-fiction.

There are, of course, in certain instances, very thin lines between the specialist and the reporter; indeed, I claim that a specialist has to be a good reporter. Some general assignment reporters, for instance, may specialize in certain subjects during part of their time; *The Times* has one such man who is a railroad "nut" who keeps up on the latest rolling equipment of the railroads of the world and who writes an occasional column about new club cars, or new wrinkles in railroading for the Sunday *Times*. The political reporter, too, is in a very real sense, a specialist in his field, though he usually confines himself to the reporting of news, rather than to its interpretation.

But you can see the trend is obvious; in the modern metropolitan newspaper it is more and more toward departmentalization of the news, and toward specialization.

I have the rare good fortune to be the military specialist of *The Times*. The special field of knowledge which my department covers happens to be of maximum interest today, but several basic fundamentals govern the work of all newspaper specialists on *The New York Times* or any other paper.

First, the specialist must have a thorough knowledge of his particular field, and it goes without saying that that knowledge must be continuously refreshed if he is to serve intelligently anything so current as the daily newspaper. Second, the specialist must be a good reporter, and third he must have judgment and analytical ability. In other words, the rôle of the specialist is something like that of the teacher; both must have a long view of history; both must interpret and explain.

Mr. Lester Markel and other speakers in this series have, I think, explained to you the difference between news, background and opinion. News is still the principal commodity of any newspaper, but modern newspapers have found it more and more necessary to provide background and interpretation, so that their readers get some continuity and some perspective and do not become hopelessly bogged down in the details of contemporary history. In many newspapers as other speakers have said, the news columns supply most of the facts; special articles and sometimes columnists plus the all-important Sunday paper provide the background and interpretation, and editorials supply the opinion.

However, in many leading metropolitan papers—and I know this is true in my own department on *The Times*—the specialist is fusing all three of these factors—facts, background and opinion—into his work, with *particular* accent upon *background and interpretation. The Times* is not a paper of columnists, and very few columnists are in reality specialists. But the late Raymond Clapper, universally respected by newspaper men, was in a real sense a specialist on the political front, and he combined in his pen and person those qualities which are essential to a specialist—knowledge, reportorial ability, judgment, a fair and analytical mind, and, when the occasion arose, emotion.

Another such columnist was the late Ernie Pyle, of whose death most of you might have read about on Okinawa today. He was killed in action as he had a premonition he would be before he went on this last mission. He was a specialist in the reporting of the GI's type of war, earnest, sincere, and with a special type of knowledge.

The job of the specialist, therefore, is in part that of a reporter. He must collect his facts like the reporter; particularly he must have wide contacts with leaders in his particular field. But he must be prepared to explain and interpret those facts and to relate them to past as well as to contemporary history.

Such are the general qualifications of the specialist, no matter whether he be a garden expert or a military editor.

I happen to be the latter, and, because I know more about my *own* job than I do about the jobs of other newspaper specialists, I would like in this final part of my talk to illustrate the work and the problems of the specialist by my own experience.

The military specialist works in a specialized field of specialization. In some ways it is a field as broad as human knowledge, for wars cannot be interpreted solely from the viewpoint of tactics and strategy; political, economic and psychological factors are often as important as military ones (and this is particularly true today in the present state of development of the war). If you look at Europe today, you will realize that as Germany dies, those factors are far more important than the ebb and flow of armies across the Rhine. In some ways it is a field sharply limited and defined; the military specialist, for instance, must know what radar is and approximately how it works; he should know the capacities and limitations of a 155 mm. gun and how many men man an assault boat.

If a communiqué states that the Elbe has been crossed, the military specialist should be able to tell his readers how military bridges are constructed, how wide and deep the Elbe is, how long it normally takes to bridge a river, etc. When the Germans invaded Norway and seized many of Norway's ports, the military specialist should have been able to draw some inferences about the chances of the British expeditionary force to Norway, inferences which would not be encouraging to the Allied cause and which would be interpreted by some readers as "pessimistic," but which could be solidly based on the known capacity and equipment of the ports available to the British.

Analytical judgment such as this—and the facts upon which that judgment is based—can be acquired by two means: personal experience, or what most of us know as the "hard school of life," and research.

Military service, therefore, is a good start toward becoming a military editor. I had the good fortune to graduate from the Naval Academy and to serve a few years in the Navy before I started my newspaper career, and after coming to *The Times* in 1929, I was given the opportunity to cover many military and naval assignments. These took me to sea with the fleet on maneuvers, into the field with the Army, and into the air with the air forces, and to all parts of the country. In 1937, Mr. Sulzberger, the far-sighted publisher of *The Times* and Mr. James, its Managing Editor, and Mr. Markel, the

Sunday Editor, realizing that military affairs, unfortunately, were destined to play a greater and greater part in our lives made me military specialist on a full-time basis, and sent me to Europe to study European armies, navies and air forces.

Since the war I have made numerous trips around the country to our training centres, and three trips overseas to various fighting fronts—once to the Pacific; once to North Africa and England, and last Summer to England and France. The job of military specialist also involves visits to Washington about once a month. For it is only by talking to all who know, and by seeing for yourself, that one can keep up with even a fraction of the information about the war. "Contacts" are the fountainhead of news and any newspaper man—whether he be reporter or specialist—must know the *men who know*, the men who *make* news. He should know these contacts— particularly the military specialist—not only as news sources but as men, for character plays a large role on the battlefield. I was fortunate, for instance, in having met some of our leaders in this war—Eisenhower, Patton, Hodges, Jonas Ingram (Commander of the Atlantic Fleet) before the war, when the spotlight of fame and glory was not upon them.

In addition to "field" knowledge, the military analyst must maintain large clipping files and a considerable library, and he must know where to find little-known, but in military operations, very important facets of knowledge. My office is a modest one; three of us work in it—my secretary, an assistant who also covers some military assignments and I. But we think we have one of the best collections of military maps, outside of the Army, in the City of New York, and we also pride ourselves on our military library. We take, read, and clip the military magazines of the world; we get the new military books, and we have many reference volumes and much source material. Many of these books and references are little known; some of them would not be found in the ordinary library.

Prior to the invasion of Okinawa, for instance, we were able to print a description of that island far more complete than any you could get from the ordinary gazeteer, geography or encyclopedia. The sources were several—a special handbook on the Pacific islands issued to a limited circle by the Navy; a book called the "Japan Pilot," reproduced by our Navy Department from British Admiralty data and procurable at hydrographic offices, and other material painfully accumulated in months and years of filing and research.

We keep also the official Army field manuals, various Navy publications, records of Congressional hearings on military and naval matters, "White Papers" and other official material issued by the British Stationery Office, and a great amount of other background material.

In addition to our own research facilities we can draw, when necessary, upon the files and library of *The Times,* upon the New York Public Library, upon Army and Navy public relations services, and—discreetly—upon the knowledge and judgment of some of my personal friends in the services.

All this information thus available is primarily, of course, background or interpretive in character, but sometimes news events make the mechanics, or the "how" of those events, assume almost as much importance in reader interest as the events themselves. For instance, when the Germans first used parachute troops in Holland in 1940, a description of the mechanics of their use—what the Army would call tactics—was published by our office, some of the facts based on information gleaned in my trip to Germany in 1937, most of them culled from authoritative articles published in "Die Wehrmacht," the "Yank" of the German Army, to which we subscribed before American entry into the war.

These examples, I think, will give you some idea of how the military specialist collects his information and goes about his job of interpreting events and supplying background to them.

This is one of his principal rôles, but it has to be done in broad strokes as well as on a small canvas. On weekdays, for instance, I may write about tanks or any of a variety of topics or about a small section of one front, thus supplying background to the news of the day. On Sunday I may try to pull together in one article all the threads of the Pacific or European wars and weave out of them an intelligible pattern.

It is this job of analysis, on a broad scale, that elicits bouquets and brickbats from readers—and sometimes from governments. Mr. James, the Managing Editor of *The Times,* gave me one exceedingly sound piece of advice when this war started—"Don't," he said, "predict."

I am reminded in this connection of the saying of Artemus Ward, the American humorist. He said: "I am not a politician, neither do I have any other vices." I say: "I am not a prophet, though I do have many other vices."

I have tried to follow that advice literally, though very occasionally I have strayed, in my interpretations, from the straight and narrow path. But even if one confines himself to an analysis of past and present events, that analysis may well please or irk many people. The military specialist bears a double cross, for if he is to be a military specialist worth his salt he *must* preserve detachment. You cannot judge battles through a rosy cloud of optimism, or a slough of pessimism; you cannot think with your stomach. Emotion in a clear-cut estimate of the situation, or in an analysis of a campaign or battle, is one of the factors to be weighed but it must be weighed clinically, coldly; a military estimate has no place for, hysteria. In other words, my purely military analyses have been based deliberately on a G-2 (which is the Army term for military intelligence) approach.

This makes some readers mad, others glad, depending on the type of mind of the reader and their individual capacity for objectivity. But pleasing the reader—or entertaining him —is not the job of the military specialist. The objective, nonpartisan approach induces some readers to call us military specialists "armchair strategists" or "generals of the typewriter"—or, as Pravda distinguished me—"admiral of the inkpool." But as in every other department of newspaper work, let me assure you that in military commentary, there are many things that don't meet the eye. You must read between the lines of the daily commentary for this background and at the moment, unprintable knowledge. "Armchair strategists," like good reporters, know things they can't, at the moment, print. This is particularly true in war, where premature publication might endanger American lives. Most military specialists knew, for instance, before the event, the approximate time and place of the North African landings. Last June, before D-Day in France, the general time of invasion could be pretty well predicted. But it was interesting to me to discover when I went aboard Admiral Kirk's and General Bradley's invasion flagship—the cruiser *Augusta* in Plymouth—that the scene of the invasion, Normandy, was about where the newspaper people had expected it would be. All this background and off-the-record knowledge keeps the specialist from "going out on a limb" and enables him to write more realistically.

I have spoken of the job of the specialist in the collection of information and of his presentation of it in background and analytical material. But the military specialist also bears upon his bowed shoulders another cross; his pieces sometimes—and not infrequently if they are to be of value—tackle controversial subjects and indulge in opinion.

Now, as you all know from this series of lectures, opinion is the kingdom of the editorial page. But from time to time opinion—honest opinion, carefully based on facts and born from judgment—is also the province of the specialist. The dramatic critic, the music critic, the motion picture editor, the business news editor, the military editor and other specialists must from time to time indulge in opinion. Any opinion

naturally must be subjective, but there are degrees of subjec-
tivity and the good specialist will try to make his opinion
reasoned and sound.

But if he thinks something is wrong—if, for instance, our
tanks are not equal in quality to the best enemy tanks—he
should say so. If he thinks a victory is not as complete as the
headlines and news stories might indicate; if—as in the case
of the Ardennes bulge battle—he is sure a defeat is being
called by some other name; he should say so, whether it is
popular or not.

Now it is obvious that an interpretation and opinion born
from any one man's brain may well differ, not only in detail
but in substance, with opinions written by anyone else. Every
specialist has had this experience; at times he may find his
analyses and opinions do not agree with the editorial opinions
which represent the official views of the paper. I know some
of the public believe—chiefly because of best-seller misinter-
pretations of the press written by people who ought to know
better—that in cases of disagreement with the paper's editorial policy the specialist trims and hedges, that he is not free
to express his honest convictions.

That has *not* been my experience and I do not believe it
has been the experience of any other specialist on *The Times*.
The Times never asks anyone to write something which he
does not believe. Nor does *The Times* prohibit the specialist
from writing what he does believe. I have written, without
fear or favor, and in freedom, although sometimes my analyses and opinions have differed with the editorial policy of
the paper. A case in point: Recently I wrote an article for
Harper's Magazine which reviewed the pros and cons of
peacetime conscription and urged a thorough study of the
subject and postponement of consideration of the legislation
until such a study will be made, possibly after the war. This
view differed from that of *The Times*. Yet many of the points
made in the *Harper's* article were previously made by me in

The Times, and I shall again discuss the subject freely when the legislation comes before Congress.

This point—the freedom of expression of the specialist, regardless of the editorial policy of the paper—is an important one, for obviously there is no use hiring a specialist if editors and publishers do not allow him to use his knowledge freely. On *The Times,* and, I think, on most other reputable American newspapers, no such problem arises.

My own views often have not been popular; I have not tried to please all of the people all of the time, some of the people all of the time, or all of the people some of the time. I have had the somewhat doubtful distinction of being bawled out in many different countries; Chungking once devoted most of a press conference to denunciation of a column I wrote; an Australian cabinet member, in polite terms called me a liar, and the Russian Army newspaper *Red Star* has depicted me in caricature in somewhat mixed company along with Dorothy Thompson and the Pope!

But such attacks have not circumscribed my freedom to tell the truth as I see it. Mr. Sulzberger, Mr. James, Mr. Markel and the management of *The Times* have consistently followed this policy in regard to specialists. It is a profoundly wise policy, a liberal policy and a sensible policy—and one which every good newspaper man instinctively appreciates. Without it specialization in newspapers is not worth the time and money.

For the specialist is interested in the same thing as all good newspapermen—the truth. Despite his specialized knowledge of his specialized field, he will make mistakes: "to err is human." But he must tell the truth as he sees it. For the truth, without fear or favor, is still the goal.

And the specialist, the reporter, the editor, the publisher, the newspaper and the school are all in pursuit of that goal.

Thomas Jefferson expressed the place of the newspaper in a democracy as well as any man before or since:

"The basis of our government being the opinion of the people," he said, "the very first object should be to keep that *right*; and were it left to me to decide whether we should have a government without newspapers or newspapers without a government, I should not hesitate a moment to prefer the latter.

"But I should intend"—he emphasized—"that every man should receive those papers, and be capable of understanding them. . . . "

That final sentence is a perpetual challenge to the *schools* and to the *press* of America.

THE JOB OF THE SPECIALIST

II

By Brooks Atkinson

Drama Critic and Correspondent. Mr. Atkinson was on the staff of the Boston Evening Transcript from 1919 to 1922. He was editor of the Book Review of The New York Times from 1922 to 1925 and was Dramatic Critic from 1925 to 1942. He served as war correspondent in China from 1942 to 1945.

IT IS MY FUNCTION to discuss newspaper criticism. Sometimes the other departments refer to us as "the trained seals"; sometimes they give it to us straight and call us "highbrows." If they were truthful they would call us anarchists, because that is what we are. At any rate, it is our mission to write the news of books, music, art, the dance, the motion pictures and the dramas. *The Times* even criticizes cooking, which shows that we understand the fundamentals of American life. Of course, newspapers do not employ critics to improve the minds of the readers nor, as far as that goes, to improve the minds of the critics, although that sometimes happens. In the baldest terms, newspapers employ critics because thousands of readers want to read a good book or see a good show. This is where criticism differs from other forms of news writing. Reporting, as a whole, is supposed to be objective—without opinion and without weighting the facts one way or another. It is humanly impossible to be objective, although there is no reason why a man shouldn't try. But criticism is subjective writing. The real news of a play is not the story, not the plot, not the characters, but the quality of the play, and whether or not it is a good play is a matter of personal opinion. Since most of my career on *The Times* until recently has been in the post of drama critic, I shall have to discuss criticism mostly in terms of the drama, although what I tell you will be, I think, more or less true of the practices of the critics of other subjects.

Producers and other theatre people who feel that they have been damaged by the critics sometimes implore the managing editors to treat the drama as a news story, that is, send a reporter to report the story of the play and record some intangible disturbance which they refer to as "audience reaction." But the story of a play usually is a pretty dull thing to read about and conveys very little information about what actually went on at the theatre last night. The news lies in the quality of the play. Was it amusing? Was it exciting? Was it moving? Did it illuminate some aspect of life? These are the things that distinguish a play from the run-of-the-mine product of the theatre. And these are all matters of personal opinion. As for "audience reaction," who can tell what that is? First Night audiences are generally composed of people who have special interest in the theatre. If they are friends of the author, or an actor or the producer, their opinion is bound to be biased. They always applaud as if the play were a masterpiece. No, I do not see how anyone can know what the audience reaction is. For a year or two, the *New York Post* used to send a reporter to the play in addition to the regular critic. The reporter was supposed to ask various members of the audience what they thought of the play. Confronted by the cosmic importance of having to express an opinion, members of the audience gave off some of the most imbecilic remarks I ever heard. It was pretty difficult to keep the audience reaction from sounding comic. After a while the *Post* abandoned this experiment. Although critics are always more or less comic figures in a democratic community that does not worship authority, I still think they make more sense than the ordinary theatregoer whose vocabulary consists of "lousy" and "swell."

At first sight, it seems reckless for a newspaper to put so much responsibility in the hands of one man. For, let's face it, what a critic says about a play in a New York newspaper has considerable influence on its commercial success or failure in the first two weeks before enough of the public has seen it to advise its friends whether to go or not. There are a number of ways to write criticism—impersonal or personal. On principle, I like them all and I think it is a salutary thing in our community to have as many different kinds of minds working on the theatre as possible. But I like best the kind of criticism that tries to look at the theatre from the audience's point of view. There is one odd thing about drama criticism. Sometimes it is a little difficult for a man to remember that he is working for a newspaper and not the theatre and that theoretically, at least, he is representing the audience. The life of the theatre is magnetic and fascinating. I don't think there are any more interesting people in the world than theatre people. They are gay, good-hearted, intelligent and imaginative. They are also hospitable. And since a critic's function is so intimately associated with the theatre, it is difficult for him not to regard himself as a theatre person and not to start seeing plays through the eyes of the theatre. When I was active as a drama critic, I used to try to go to the theatre with no more idea of what I was going to see than a layman. I did not read the reviews of the preliminary engagements out-of-town. I tried to hear as little gossip as possible about plays that were coming in, for it seemed to me the important thing was to see a play as anybody else might come to see it, in the hope of a good evening in the theatre.

Probably criticism is a pompous word to apply to theatre reviewing. It should be known as "reviewing." We are popularly referred to as "critics." But I have always thought that it would be closer to the truth to describe us as "reviewers." Criticism of the drama would be a much more profound thing. A real critic should follow a play through all the experiences it undergoes before it reaches the public. For instance, a real critic ought to read the script as it comes from the author's hands. He ought to know why a certain director has been chosen to stage the script, because the script begins to undergo transformation as soon as the director begins to have ideas about it. Then the critic should know why the various actors are chosen. Obviously, the choice of actors has a tremendous effect on the script. Invariably, the author and the director are unable to get the actors they want. Invariably, they have to find actors, at least for the subordinate rôles, that are not their first choice. Finally, a critic should attend the rehearsals, or at least some of the rehearsals. In order to understand thoroughly the whole quality of the final stage product he should have this intimate acquaintance with the whole magic process that results in an acted play. I think this would be something you could honestly call "criticism." But, of course, it would not represent an audience point of view. No newspaper could hire enough critics to deal with plays in this exhaustive fashion. And it is not certain that what they wrote would be of much use in a daily newspaper. Once, as an experiment, I almost took a crack at this kind of criticism. Jed Harris, a very volatile person, as you probably know, and I, several times discussed this kind of criticism. We agreed that I should attend some of the rehearsals of his next play, so that when it finally opened I should know something about its background. When he had the first act in pretty good shape, I went to see it. I found it terribly moving. I liked it enormously; in fact, it seemed to be so much the kind of play I like that I was afraid of knowing too much about it before it opened and of losing my first rapturous impressions. The play was called "Our Town." After seeing that one rehearsal of the first act, I kept away from it until it finally opened at Henry Miller's theatre. For what I wanted to get out of that play was the enjoyment of seeing it for the first time from a seat in the theatre.

Perhaps you will be interested in the technique or, shall we say, craftsmanship of play reviewing. I shall naturally have to speak for myself. Other critics do the job differently. Lewis Nichols, who is now drama critic for *The Times*, is a fast man with a typewriter and can hit a deadline right on the nose. As a thinking and writing machine he operates much better than I do, and those are essential qualities of a good newspaper man. But, as I have said, I shall have to speak for myself. When I am in the theatre as a critic I try to see the play as other people are seeing it, but of course, I am always aware of the fact that I have got to write something about it when the play is over. I suppose I am always trying to think of what I am going to say. Sometimes I scrawl words on the program—bits of dialogue that I want to remember and words to describe the actors. Contrary to a popular superstition, almost all critics almost invariably remain until the play is over. Sometimes plays are so terrible that it would be torture to expect anybody to stay through the last act. But that does not happen more than two or three times in a season. It is no breach of faith to leave most musical shows by eleven or eleven-fifteen. By that time, everyone knows whether they are good or not. And since musical shows are likely to run until eleven-thirty or sometimes later, a reviewer would have very little time to write his notice if he stayed until the end. But a drama is not complete until the final curtain, and except in the unusual circumstances I have already described, it would not be fair to leave before the end. But the instant the curtain begins to fall, you will see the critics racing for the street in the hope of getting out before the exits are clogged with people who have nothing more to do except to drop in somewhere for a drink and then go home. A. B. Walkley, the eminent critic of the *London Times*, once said that the first sentence in a review is the important one. If the first sentence is right, the rest of the review falls into place very nicely. But if the first sentence is wrong, nothing a writer can do will make the review coherent and lucid. That has been my experience, too. So in the few minutes during which I hustle back to the office I always try to get the first sentence in my mind. I find that I can write more rapidly and better in pencil than I can on the typewriter. That is a habit that distresses the compositors, but over a period of years they have learned how to cope with it. In the first paragraph of the review I have always tried to summarize the whole play—suggest what kind of a play it is, what it is about, and who is in it and how well they do. By the time the first paragraph is written there is a copy boy at the office to take it to the copy desk where a sympathetic scholar examines it for accuracy and to censor any furtive suggestions of obscenity; and he in turn sends the copy to the composing room. Meanwhile, I am writing the second paragraph which is usually a brief sketch of the story and the copy boy takes this as he did the first paragraph. The third paragraph is generally a critical discussion of the play and the last paragraphs are discussions of the acting. By this time, the first parts of the review are already set in type and proofs have been taken of them. In another fifteen minutes or so, the last paragraphs are also set and after the proofs have been corrected there is not much a man can do except go home and go to bed.

People who have been damaged or think they have been damaged by criticism frequently say that it is unfair for a critic to pass judgment in an hour or so on a piece of work that has been a month or two in the mill. They say that a critic can destroy in an hour something that thirty or forty people have spent weeks trying to create That is a plausible argument, and seems particularly plausible when they go on to say that a critic should wait until the next day before he writes his review. But there are two or three answers to that.

In the first place, how long does it take you to make up your mind whether you like or dislike a play? You know as soon as the final curtain falls. In the second place, theatre is, in one degree or another, exciting. And I think a review conveys more of the theatre when it is written in the heat of excitement just after the curtain has fallen. Since Sunday editions go to press somewhat earlier than the week-day editions it is customary to postpone reviews of Saturday night openings until the Monday paper. I always used to find that it was drudgery to try to recapture on Sunday afternoon, the excitement, if any, that I got in the theatre on Saturday night. It is a rare play that it still exciting after a night's sleep and the distractions of reading the Sunday morning newspapers. When St. John Ervine was the guest critic on the old *World*, fifteen years ago, he published his reviews two days after the play opened. That turned out to be an unsatisfactory schedule, although it is fair to say that the experiment was handicapped by the fact that all the other critics were following the usual practice of writing their reviews for the next day's paper.

And now, as to the tradition that critics kill plays. Frankly, I doubt it. There are too many instances of plays with popular appeal that have succeeded without the support of most of the critics, like "Abie's Irish Rose" and "Tobacco Road" and "Hell's-a-poppin'." I can't think of any plays that failed in the face of unanimously favorable reviews by the critics, but I know from bitter experience about plenty of plays that I have liked that the public has refused to accept—like "Rainbow," a fabulously enjoyable musical show that lasted only a couple of weeks; Sean O'Casey's "Within the Gates" that never really made both ends meet; also a very moving and honest play called "The World We Make" that failed ignominiously four or five years ago; and Saroyan's first play, "My Heart's in the Highlands," a fresh, lyrical drama that should have had a long run, except that the public didn't want it. I think I could tell you of more plays I liked that failed than of plays I disliked that succeeded. For audiences have an inscrutable genius for making up their minds about plays without the benefit of newspaper criticism.

If a play can survive two or three weeks at the box-office, it is in the hands of the public. Nothing a critic can say one way or another will have much effect on it. And so, I have always maintained that it is not the critics who kill plays but the authors who do not write good ones and the directors who do not stage them intelligently or the actors who do not play them well. If it is the critics who are responsible for failures in the theatre, then logically, it is the critics who are responsible for the successes. But no one believes that; everyone knows that successes in the theatre are made, not by the critics who are sitting in the audience, but the authors who write good scripts, and the directors and actors who present them to the audience beautifully.

I should like now to go off the deep end and talk a little about art. The backbone of the theatre business is amusement. It always has been; that is a legitimate function of the theatre. But what gives the theatre its reputation and prestige are the works of art that occasionally it creates. Theatre reviewing would be a deadly trade if there were no art in the theatre. The greatest privilege a reviewer has is to recognize a work of art when it appears and to say something in praise of it. By "art" I do not mean something precious or priggish, for there is art in nearly every aspect of human life. Leonardo da Vinci said that the subject of art is "man and the hopes of his soul." The only definition of art that ever satisfied me was Emerson's. He said: "Art is the mixture of man's will with nature." In other words, a desk like this one is art. The nature in it is the wood that came from a tree. The art is the shape some man has given to it. The purpose of the desk is to provide a shelf on which a man can read or write and store papers, books and whatever he needs. Those functions could be satisfied by a standard design. But the infinite variety of man's will is revealed in the infinite variety of desk designs that you encounter everywhere. Some desks are big, plain and massive, without embellishment; some are delicate, with rare curves, beautiful mouldings, and carvings; every period in history, every nationality has produced a different desk. For man's will has an untold number of manifestations. And you cannot extinguish his aspirations. Once you begin to look at art from this point of view, you find that life is tingling with hope and ideas, and you realize that the finest art of all is the art of living. As you walk along the street, observing how people dress and behave, or look into windows and see how people try to relieve the monotony of life by a little variation in the patterns of their existence, you find that, after all, life is a very exhilarating process and you are very glad to be alive.

This may seem remote from the theatre, but it is not. The theatre is a more compact and magnetic form of art than ordinary living. It has ideas, it has imagination, it has beauty, and unlike life in the raw, it has form. One of the finest things about the theatre is the fact that, at least comparatively, theatre people are free spirits. They have nothing at stake but the truth. By and large the serious dramatists are progressive and liberal in their attitude towards life. They like to be leaders of thought. And they have a sense of public responsibility. Sometimes this is a little tiresome to people who want to go to the theatre just for a good time. I remember towards the end of the 1930's when the world seemed to be slipping crazily into war, the theatre broke out in rash of plays about democracy. Not very many of them were good, because ideas in the theatre are not much good unless they grow out of human characters. Being a popular form of art, the theatre does not have much use for abstract ideas. But it seems to me the thing that makes the theatre worth while is the fact that it attracts so many people with good ideas who are constantly trying to share them with the public. Real art is illumination. It gives a man an idea he never had before or lights up ideas that were formless or only lurking in the shadows of his mind. It adds stature to life. In the course of a New York season we are lucky if we have one or two plays of this caliber, and if we have eight or ten plays that stimulate the mind. But that's enough. No one expects to add a cubit to his stature every time he goes into the theatre. From the point of view of a newspaper, it is news and good news, too, when a fine play comes along. It has always seemed to me remarkable that the public acts on the news so quickly. By noon of the next day there will be a line of people at the box office. For people are very eager to get good news about the theatre. It is the function of a newspaper to print the bad news as well as the good, impartially. But I think I can speak for all reviewers when I say that there is no joy so great as that of reporting that a good play has come to town.

CHAPTER EIGHT

THE NEWSPAPER'S ROLE IN THE COMMUNITY

By Arthur Hays Sulzberger

Publisher of the New York Times. Mr. Sulzberger joined the staff of The Times in 1919, as assistant to the Publisher, the late Adolph S. Ochs. He became Publisher on May 7, 1935.

I AM GLAD TO WELCOME YOU here today and regret that illness has prevented my attending all of these sessions. Now that we start on the last, all of you must realize how much remains to be covered. For my assignment is not only to talk to you of the rôle of the newspaper in the community but to speak of those departments of this newspaper which have not been represented here. It is my hope, during the course of these remarks, to answer as many of the questions as I can which have been asked but left unanswered. I shall try, too, to reply to some of those that have been hurled at us silently or, at least, with no noise except the rustle of newsprint by the regular attendant who devotes his time at these meetings to a thorough reading of *PM*.

As to our rôle in the community—I think I can answer that very simply in the words of Adolph S. Ochs, about whom I should like to talk to you briefly. Born in Cincinnati, Ohio, of parents who had fled Germany in the revolution of 1848, he came to New York in 1896 to take over a majority interest and the control of the then moribund *New York Times*, just as in 1878, at the age of twenty, he had taken over a half interest in *The Times* of Chattanooga, Tenn. In that early venture he had risked $250, a large sum from the family exchequer for which, even at that age, he was chiefly responsible. In New York his reorganization scheme, which was accepted by those who had long since placed the property in an oxygen tent—called for an investment of $75,000. The difference between that sum and the value of the controlling interest in *The New York Times* that you now see is accounted for by the earnings plowed back into the paper by this man who knew how to publish a good newspaper and also make it pay.

I dwell on this because one hears a lot about newspaper barons and lords of the press. Well, there are some who might have called Adolph Ochs one of those when he died, but he didn't start as one, and competition in his early days in the New York newspaper field was just about as tough as it is now. Men accurately described as millionaires were contesting for supremacy. Hearst and Pulitzer and Bennett were not pikers—yet $75,000 and the man who knew how to make a newspaper built *The New York Times*.

When he took over, he published one of what I believe were the only two statements that ever appeared in this paper over his signature, in which he dedicated this property "to give all the news without fear or favor, regardless of any party, sect or interest involved." That remains its rôle in the community—to give the news; and I don't suppose there are many in this audience or elsewhere who question that it succeeds. I take it that what we are interested in today is to see if we are performing our allotted task accurately, and without fear, and without favor.

We recognize that there is no way to recapture the past, with the printed word or in any other manner, that will be satisfactory to all.

We know that if each one of you were to report the same event there would be many different versions.

We know that a verbatim report of proceedings is not the answer, even if it were possible to print that much and find those who would read it. That fact was driven home to me some years ago when Franklin Roosevelt made a speech and the news lay not in what he said but in the political significance of the fact that, for the first time in his amazing career, he had a cool reception. The news on that particular night would have escaped a stenographic record.

We know that all men have their prejudices, their predilections, their special interests or biases and, accordingly, we would not put the writing and editing of the news into the hands of any single group—political, economic, religious or social.

We would not knowingly employ any so-called Communist, or any other kind of totalitarian, in our news or editorial departments, for we have a deep-rooted prejudice for democracy and a deep-seated faith in our capacity to develop under a system of law.

On the other hand, we believe that trained and skilled newspaper men and women, such as you have seen here, who have no common denominator other than their Americanism, have the ability to write and evaluate a news story that will be acceptable to most of our readers as an accurate report of what transpired. I stress that this is for our readers—not for all; for every newspaper must decide upon the clientele it wishes to cultivate.

For our part, we solicit the patronage of intelligent Americans, who desire information rather than entertainment, who want the facts unadorned and who, in this critical period of our history, place first their country and the freedoms which it guarantees.

We do not crusade in our news columns.

We are anxious to see wrongs corrected, and we attempt to make our position very clear in such matters on our editorial page. But we believe that no matter how we view the world, our chief responsibility lies in reporting accurately that which happens.

Whichever way the cat may jump, we should record it, and we should not allow our excitement about the direction which it takes, or plans to take, to interfere with our primary mission. We believe that you will look after the cat if we inform you promptly, fully and accurately about its movements.

We have never had a single advertiser attempt to shape our editorial policy, although it is not uncommon for an occasional one to show disapproval of them by withdrawing his business. Every election year is apt to bring a flare-up of this manifestation, but, despite stupid and vicious remarks to the contrary, we take it in our stride and pursue our course.

We are not afraid of advertisers, but maintain a normal, friendly business relationship with them.

We maintain a committee of acceptability of advertising and subject copy to its scrutiny. In normal years we turn down many thousands of lines of business which does not comply with our standards and, in addition, require the advertiser to edit some of that which we use.

We are financially independent.

We have no investments except in our own business and in Government securities.

We have no mortgages or bonds outstanding—no debts other than our monthly bills. The majority stock of The New York Times Company is held by three trustees, all of whom are employed on *The Times*. There is no outside interference.

We have no temptation to be other than honest.

We have no wish except to hold high the banner of responsible journalism raised by Mr. Ochs and held aloft by him until his death ten years ago.

Now, who is this "we" that I have been talking about? In the first place, *The New York Times*, a newspaper, is published by The New York Times Company, a corporate entity—a "we" before the law. We have a payroll of more than $170,000 a week and employ full time more than 2,500 persons. We have the business problems that other corporations have. We pay taxes; we engage in collective bargaining; we obey the fire laws and building codes; and we do not feel that freedom of the press is infringed upon when we do.

As in every other business, there are officers, a board of directors and stockholders. As in every other business, the president or chairman of the board is the head. In this particular business the position of publisher also carries great responsibilities. He has the power to employ the chief executives, the *power* to put anything into the paper, or take anything out that he wishes; and on *The Times,* the offices of publisher, president and chairman of the board are all held by me. That is a lot of power to place in the hands of any individual. So, let's take it to pieces, see how it happened and what it means, for certainly it is a matter of public concern.

For many years your students and others have been asking me how to succeed in the newspaper business, and my answer on many occasions has been: "Work hard, never watch the clock, polish the handle on the big front door and marry the boss's daughter!" That's what I did in 1917. Mr. Ochs had one child and she is now Mrs. Sulzberger, and I came to *The Times* when I got out of the army at the end of the last war. When Mr. Ochs died, he left in trust the controlling stock of this company for the benefit of his grandchildren, who happen to be Mrs. Sulzberger's children and mine. He named three trustees—General Adler, who opened this series of meetings, Mrs. Sulzberger, who conceived them, and myself; and the fact that Mrs. Sulzberger and I get along pretty well explains my being publisher of *The New York Times.* It is no more complicated than that!

As I told a group some time ago, however, please don't assume that by the mere exercise on my part of the powers to which I have referred *The New York Times* can be produced. Quite the contrary is the case. Persons of the caliber that have addressed you at these meetings are not yes men. They are trained, independent newspaper people who joined the staff of *The New York Times* because they knew Mr. Ochs practiced, and desired to have practiced, what he preached; and they had sufficient confidence in his integrity to know that in that kind of an organization they could exercise their talents freely and without restraint. The motto "All the News That's Fit to Print" is in their hearts as well as on the masthead of the paper.

Some forty years ago, Charles R. Miller, then editor of *The New York Times,* described a newspaper as "not what men make it from day to day." "There is a genius of continuance," he said, "that guides their pens and policies, and through the rolling years throws the steady light of individual character and consistent purpose upon the printed page." It is that "genius of continuance" that is the fundamental "we" that I have been talking about. And my associates will tell you that their loyalty is to that something that is "we," of which they are a part. Some years ago it was Hearst's *American* and Pulitzer's *World,* but it never was Ochs' *Times* —only *The Times*; and it is *The Times* today, with each one of us who works here owing allegiance to the spirit that is it.

Now, having said all that, I assume your first question would be, "How do you reach an editorial decision to support a particular candidate, let us say? Do you take a show of hands? Must it be unanimous and, if not, how are the votes counted?"

Let me give you an example of what happened in 1940. Mr. Roosevelt, whom all of us now mourn, was running for his third term against Mr. Willkie. We supported Mr. Willkie. Before that time the three trustees of the controlling stock, whom I have named, had always voted Democratic in national elections. That year they all voted for Mr. Willkie, as did the chief executives, including the editor in charge of the editorial page. Of the staff that contributes to that page, some twelve in number, eight voted for Mr. Willkie, three for Mr. Roosevelt, and one remains to this day a secret ballot. That's the record of election day, 1940.

But I would maintain that no other course could have been expected by those who read our editorial page. In times of peace a newspaper has few secrets. Its business is to tell what it knows and how it feels. And we had been telling quite consistently that we didn't like the effort to pack the Supreme Court; that we did not like the third term; that we did not like the President's expressed desire to send Congress home and run the country as a one man show without it.

We believe that our record was entirely consistent and that our support of the great liberal, Wendell Willkie, should have been foreseen just as, conversely, our support in 1944 of Mr. Roosevelt should have been evident to a reader of our editorial page. During the war years he had gallantly upheld the position of our country in the world; and, after Mr. Willkie had been passed over by the Republicans, and Mr. Dewey in his speeches had failed to excoriate sufficiently the isolationists in his party, who had done their best to obstruct the passage of lend-lease, universal military service and other legislation in which we believed, the direction in which we were to throw our support should have been evident.

The control that the publisher of this paper exercises over its policies is anything but arbitrary. It lies primarily in picking his associates and working with them in harmony— talking things out and, on many occasions, being willing to give *way* rather than give *orders*.

I do not wish to appear naive or sentimental in this matter. I merely assure you, out of twenty-seven years' experience, that you could not have a newspaper as good as this one if what I have outlined were not so.

Now, if I may, let me retrace and take up some of the

points that I have merely touched on and which, from past experience, I judge to be of interest to you. I will not burden you with statistics or charts, or go into the intricacies of production, other than to say that about 50 per cent of the people who work here are employed in the mechanical departments—the processes that convert the typewritten copy into type and from that type print and distribute the many thousands of newspapers that compose our circulation. I mention this only to draw attention to the fact that the cost of these processes, when the raw paper is included, is about four-fifths of our total expense—and yet, all that you have heard about is the other fifth. That is as it should be. It is the brain and not the body that concerns you; but I, who have jurisdiction over five-fifths, would like to assure you that this body contains a heart, and that in labor matters we try to follow the advice which, in our editorial columns, we offer to others.

Now let me come back to that question of the control of those columns which, very naturally, in view of all the misstatements, are uppermost in many minds. Our income from circulation last year (and all my figures are for 1944) was some $7,000,000, or slightly less than one third of our total. The balance of our revenue, aside from investments, is derived from advertising. This advertising revenue, in turn, can be broken down roughly as follows: 24 per cent comes from classified advertising; 46 per cent from national, and 30 per cent from retail. Now, the classified income came from approximately one million and a quarter individual advertisers or, it would be better to say, that number of individual advertisements—since if you are looking for a maid in these days it may be necessary to repeat the same advertisement forever.

Our national business represents many thousands of separate advertisers who have no association but are scattered about the country. Only in the retail group, which accounts for less than one-third of our business, could you pick out, say, twenty-five merchants who might hope by economic pressure to influence the freedom of our editorial expression. Well, I admit they might try it, but I can tell you very definitely that they have never done so; and I would point out further that since these are advertisers who deal directly with a mass of consumers, every business instinct must suggest to them the avoidance of interference in matters on which their customers differ.

I have gone into this at length, for I should like to knock down once and for all the fallacious notion that advertisers are a venal influence upon editorial policies and point out, conversely, that it isn't the advertising but the lack of advertising of which you should be fearful. When advertising revenue is nonexistent or insufficient, as was conspicuously the case in France before the war, then watch out! Except in the rarest cases, such a paper has been supported by subvention of *some* sort. It is to the interest of *someone*, or *some* group, to keep it alive for *some* purpose, and "caveat emptor" would be the proper slogan to put in the little box on the front page that we call the ear.

We have one additional important rôle in the community. It is ours by default, however, because you and the rest of the public fail to understand that it is yours rather than ours. I refer to freedom of the press and to the protection of that freedom.

The conventions that met in Philadelphia from 1787–89 were not gatherings of newspaper publishers; nor was there any pressure group from the American Newspaper Publishers Association to force the first amendment into the Constitution, or to include the press in that amendment as one of the four fundamental freedoms upon which we build our lives. In fact, there was a good deal of argument as to whether or not it should be included, although its importance was never questioned.

Alexander Hamilton wrote in *The Federalist*: "What signifies a declaration, that 'the liberty of the press shall be inviolably preserved'? What is the liberty of the press? Who can give it definition which would not leave the utmost latitude for evasion? I hold it to be impracticable; and from this I infer that its security, whatever fine declaration may be inserted in any constitution respecting it, must altogether depend on public opinion, and on the general spirit of the people and of the government."

Jefferson, who took issue with Hamilton, argued that a strong central government might seek to abuse its power; that it was necessary to protect the *citizen* from such abuse; and the first amendment to the Bill of Rights, including freedom of the press, is attributable to his insistence. If you add habeas corpus to that list of freedoms, as was done by our constitutional assembly, we have the base upon which to build a land where there shall be freedom from want and freedom from fear as well as many affirmative blessings for mankind.

What I would point out to you is that freedom of the press is your right as citizens and not mine as a publisher. Mr. Hamilton, in his way, was right in contending that freedom of the press must depend on public opinion. The newspapers of Germany continued to make money long after they had lost their freedom, but freedom of the individual died in Germany the day that freedom of the press perished. How often must it happen? Wherever the press is controlled by government, the other fundamental freedoms go; just as human beings go behind barbed wire—go mysteriously, with only a rude knocking on the door at midnight.

All of our citizenry would be prompt to defend any attack upon freedom of speech, religion or assembly. But the throne of liberty is four-legged, and freedom of the press is the fourth and completes its structure. My plea to you teachers is to drive home that truth. I urge you not to fear being bromidic. In the words of the Old Testament, rather, I would say: "These words shall be in thine heart; and thou shalt teach them diligently unto thy children; and shalt talk of them when thou sittest in thine house, and when thou walkest by the way, and when thou liest down, and when thou risest up."

And I would like to add that unless you do so—unless *we* make everyone conscious of the fact that freedom of the press is a protection for himself rather than for newspapers —then tyranny from within may one day overrun us and all those we now mourn shall have died in vain. Do not let the actions of some publishers divert you from your task. Remember that freedom of the press means the freedom to print what they will. It means your freedom to circulate a handbill if we, in our freedom, refuse to print that which you would have us say. For such refusal on our part could be an aspect of a "free" press. It would not, however, meet any definition of a "responsible" press, and that is what we are achieving in this country—a responsible press built upon the structure of freedom—a press that admits that the way it presents the news is a matter of legitimate public concern.

For that reason you are entitled to know more of how we handle the news, or, to phrase it better, how we deal with some of the exceptional cases that come to us, since it is the exception that so frequently tests policy. Before the war, I know of only one instance where policy affected us and a fear of consequences caused us to deviate from a strict news presentation. That was when the Bank of United States was failing. We were told that night that there was one faint chance that the bank might open the next morning. We decided that we would censor ourselves and not tell all we knew rather than be the cause of closing the bank after it opened, and thereby inflict untold suffering and loss on its depositors. In fact, we had an account of over $16,000 in that bank which we did not withdraw for the same reason. Maybe it was wrong. Perhaps we should never have deviated from our rule to tell all we know; but these years of war have made me think that we were right in 1930.

Since the start of the war, however, it has been a different story. We have been in possession of much unpublished information, and secrets have been guarded because the security of the country was involved. We have known where the President was when he was on secret missions. We know the contents of the still secret famous letter which Ambassador Davies carried from the President to Marshal Stalin. We have known the dates and spots chosen for some of our invasions. We have known some of the past strains between the Allies. We have had fuller reports of the meetings of the so-called Big Three than were made public. We have known our weaknesses when they were great, and now know something of our still undisclosed strength. We have known about sinkings before they were announced, the movement of troops and the location of individual units. But is this really important at this time? You might have curiosity about some of these questions, but you wouldn't really want to know about many of them. It's a burden—a terrible burden to carry a secret on which so much, so many may depend. I assure you I have practiced forgetting as I have traveled around the world these last few years, and I have specifically refrained from asking questions which would have been answered.

That must not continue when the fighting stops, however. The community is adult and is entitled to the facts on which to base its judgment and form its action. If for no other reason, we must hasten the end of war so that you may again become the full masters of your destiny.

Questions are sometimes asked about our headlines—about the position that we give to a story in the paper and the amount of space we allot to it. May I recall that Mr. James told you that we receive nightly more than a million words, and then add, as Mr. MacNeil pointed out—that there are no headlines on any of the material when received. We have to read all of that copy, select from it, edit it and write those headlines; and not only must we put the essence of a story into those heads, but we are obliged to confine ourselves to a limited number of individual characters to each line, and that number varies with the type of headline that we determine upon. It stands to reason that a margin of error must be counted on by us. It follows equally that what may suit us will not appeal to all as representing accurately what they may construe as the important part of the news story.

Realize, too, that after we have put into the paper those stories that the editors have selected as important, many of the short pieces that you see are chosen because of their size. The make-up editor places the type in the chase, which is nothing more than a metal frame in which a page of type is locked before the first reproducing and manifold process starts. In that chase, let us say, there is an empty space of three inches in depth. The make-up editor has before him in type the shorter stories that have already passed the copy-readers. He chooses from them a story that will fit the space, or possibly two that will add up to the space he has available. At this point it is primarily an arithmetic problem rather than an editorial choice.

Editorial choice, however, is at the bottom of all we are discussing. Given a management which determined in these days of limited newsprint paper to print last year 15,000 more columns of news than any other newspaper (and at 300 lines to a column that means sacrificing 4,500,000 lines of advertising to give this service); given a management that permits the unshackled functioning of the editors' talents, the judgment of the community will still rest upon the judgment of the editors who actually put the paper to bed each night. That is the reason why we want good news men who recognize a good news story, just as a judge of horse flesh recognizes a good horse. We want men of varied creeds and varied backgrounds. We don't count noses to see how many of each, but we refuse to limit any. As an example, we have consistently refused to turn over exclusively to members of the Newspaper Guild the writing and editing of the news. We have opposed their guild shop or closed shop demands, and will continue to do so. We would oppose such demands even if the Guild represented all labor instead of merely one wing of a warring labor movement.

May I add at this point that our opposition is not directed to unions or closed shops in general—we have many in our industry. We oppose a closed shop vigorously, however, in our news department and we do so for the protection of the public.

We are aware, and you should be, that a news story always runs the risk of giving a one-sided picture because news is generally a departure from the normal. It may be good; it may be bad; it may be the discovery of penicillin; it may be murder—for when a man kills his wife it's news; when he kisses her it isn't. If a strike is called, we report it daily, but if no strike is on it does not constitute a news story every day that there is no strike. It only become news when a considerable period of time has elapsed without strikes, and then someone calls attention to the fact that for such and such a time no strike has occurred to impede the war effort.

These are some of the difficulties in reporting and presenting the news that I hope you will bear in mind.

Dr. Wade, Dr. Greenberg and you, Ladies and Gentlemen—we on *The New York Times* are deeply appreciative of the trust you have shown in us. If you have profited as much as we, this experiment has been a success, for I assure you that this course has given to us a fresh insight into our own responsibilities. If you, in turn, have been helped, there can be cause for mutual satisfaction. We thank you and stand ready to assist in your discussion groups.

The United States of America is a great country, and ours is a great responsibility, for we have been the privileged ones—not only during this war but long before. It is a heritage of freedom, not the establishment or recapture of freedom, for which we fight.

If we should share this blessing, there is no better way to do so than to assure the free flow of news and free access to the news in all lands. Then those who have been newly freed can learn and profit by our experience. For if our country can hold true to our faith and sustain our precious freedoms —all of them—it is not too much to hope that what we now see and hear in the world is not the agony of death but the birth pains of humanity's freedom.

REPORT OF TEACHERS'
DISCUSSIONS

REPORT OF TEACHERS' DISCUSSIONS

BASED ON

THE NEW YORK TIMES LECTURES

COMPILED BY

ISAAC BILDERSEE

Principal, Seth Low Junior High School,
Brooklyn, N. Y.

AFTER THE CONCLUSION of the lectures at Times Hall, some two hundred teachers registered in the discussion groups, or "workshop groups" as they were called, to continue the study of the place of the daily newspaper in our public schools. An attempt was made to arrange membership in these groups on the basis of similarity of interests and teaching positions, but we were not entirely succeessful in this because of the wide diversity of teaching and other professional occupations represented. Teachers upon all levels of school organization were among the participants, as well as clerks, social service workers, and others even less directly connected with classroom instruction.

An interesting and informative experience afforded to each group was a guided visit through *The Times* plant. The understanding thus obtained of the enormously complicated processes involved in the production of a newspaper, from the reception of news bulletins to the loading of the delivery trucks, enhanced for the teachers and in consequence for their pupils, the appreciation of the daily paper.

The assignment given to each of these workshops was, primarily, to evaluate the advantages of using the daily paper as a vehicle of instruction, and, of equal importance, to study the limitations and possibly detrimental influences involved. The actual experience of the teachers was sought so that in the interchange of thought all might profit by the successes and the failures of other members of the groups. Suggestions were sought also, for the improvement of approaches and techniques, not emanating from experiences already known, and possibly for modifications in newspaper editing and publishing that might enhance the value of the paper to the children in the schools.

Each of the workshop groups submitted a record of its proceedings as a final report. It is obvious that among these reports there would, of necessity, be a great deal of duplication of statement and of suggestion. The task of selecting the various items presented in the reports and of organizing the resulting material upon a reasonably coherent basis has been a complicated one. The assembled digest of these reports is presented as a guide to those who may seek information and suggestions concerning the use of the newspaper in class.

The changing point-of-view, as indicated in these reports, is worth recording. Several years ago, at a luncheon conference presided over by the genial Dr. Finley, the function of the newspaper in the classroom was conceived by the teachers present only as an adjunct to the teaching of various school subjects. The suggestion that we abandon that attitude and recognize the importance of developing an appreciation of the daily paper of and for itself, an understanding of newspaper standards, with an accompanying cultivation of good judgment in selecting papers and skill in using them was received with polite skepticism. The acquisition of accurate information is an essential objective, of course, in all philosophies of education. But with newer concepts of the means by which usable information is acquired and retained, has come a fuller understanding of the function of integrating experiences as the basis of learning. The daily paper is probably the most potent approach to this integration in the lives of an overwhelming majority of our people. It is natural, therefore, that it should be accorded, in itself, an important area in school experience, and that its function as a tool for the assimilation of material in other fields, however important, should become a secondary, though still important, consideration.

Discussion of the use of the newspaper, in the eleven workshop groups, included references to many objectives, diverse subject areas, and all levels of pupil maturity. The time allotted was far too short to permit the comprehensive treatment that all concerned thought should be given to the topic. Very little thought, for example, was given to the techniques of delivery and distribution, of use of the daily paper in the lowest grades, of the paper as a model and a guide to pupils engaged in the project of publishing a class or a school periodical. These topics, it is to be hoped, will merit fuller discussion in a future section of the course planned tentatively for a later school term.

It is difficult to select from the reports rendered, the outstanding thoughts crystallizing from the discussion. Any recapitulation, however, would include the following postulates, each of which is discussed briefly in the paragraphs that follow.

1. The daily paper is a significant factor in the development of pupil character;
2. The daily paper is a significant element in the background of pupil experience;
3. The daily paper is, in itself, a subject for study.
4. The daily paper may exert a wholesome influence in helping the pupil achieve his start in post-school life;
5. The daily paper is an invaluable tool in the guidance of pupil learning in virtually all subject areas of school instruction;

6. The daily paper is of value on all levels of pupil experience, increasingly so with the approach to maturity;
7. The daily paper is of maximum service when its use is carefully programmed, and adequate provision is made for delivery and distribution.

I. THE DEVELOPMENT OF CHARACTER

In all eleven of the workshop group reports, primary emphasis, expressed or implicit, was placed on the development of desirable character attributes among the pupils. The most frequently mentioned of these traits of personality is awareness of the events in the world beyond the schoolroom, interest in affairs transcending the petty interests of the individuals, alertness to the events and changes recorded in the daily paper. A teacher of shorthand, for example, reporting for workshop 10, says, "It would be most intelligent of the teachers of all subjects to do as much as possible towards building the well-rounded citizen; and his primary requirement is to be aware of what is going on in the world around him."

Effective citizenship is seen as an outcome of newspaper reading. The report of Group 5 lists the outcomes to be achieved as:

1. "active interest in civic affairs;
2. "better informed body of citizens;
3. "intelligent and discerning consumer body;
4. "critical evaluation of issues;
5. "responsible community leadership."

The same point-of-view is expressed in the report of Group 6. "One of the most important uses of the newspaper is to discuss and interpret the news as it affects democratic institutions."

Good citizenship, however, cannot be acquired merely through reading and discussion. Worthy attitudes of participation and leadership in community affairs are the outgrowths of developing services in the widening circles of individual membership and interest. Responsibility to the smaller community, the family, the class, the school, prepares the way for the wider responsibilities of the adult. Stress is laid in various reports upon the importance of this functional approach to the development of desirable attitudes through pupil responsibilities in such matters as receiving and distributing the papers, preparing reports individually or in committee, collecting topical material for clipping collections, scrap-books, and similar purposes—useful to the class and to the school.

Closely allied to the good citizenship traits of character are the power and habit of critical thinking. Several of the groups emphasize this outcome of newspaper reading, considering it a primary value, from which others are evolved. Thus, Group 5 reports as an outstanding result to be achieved:

The development of critical attitudes:

1. "Discrimination in the selection of reading matter;
2. "Evaluation of news and background material;
3. "Questioning spirit towards opinions expressed in newspapers;
4. "Aesthetic appreciation of format and makeup of paper;
5. "Appreciation of the newspaper as a civic and social force in the community."

In other groups similar conclusions were reached, the emphasis being placed on the withholding of judgment in matters involving differences of opinion. It is suggested by various groups, for example, that news reports in dailies of varying trends of editorial attitude be read and compared, that all pertinent factual information be assembled and evaluated, before even tentative expressions of opinion be attempted. It is agreed by all that the opinions and judgments reached be those of the pupils—not those of either the editor or the teacher. Group 2 proposed a series of questions to evaluate the usefulness and the success of the use of the newspaper in class, one of them, "Have we encouraged the children to express their opinions?" To this we might add, Have we insisted the opinions be the outcome of carefully considered information?

A further distinguishing trait of good character is the acceptance of every member of the community for his personal worth and achievement—the one characteristic of democratic living common to all the varied concepts and definitions. Group 3 includes in the program of effective use of the newspaper:

"Promotion of racial good will through admiration of prominent figures of all races and nationalities."

Group 5 urges "Emphasis on social and civic leaders in diversified groups."

The wise employment of leisure time as an index of individual interests frequently is an index of effective character. This idea is expressed in the report of various groups that see in developing habits of newspaper reading the effective use of time that might otherwise be spent in fruitless indolence or, at best, in passive reception of entertainment afforded by the radio or the motion picture. A more discriminating enjoyment of these amenities of our civilization may be developed through newspaper reading, especially of critiques by competent staff members. Hobbies may be developed and fostered—photography, stamp collecting, plant cultivation, household arts, pets—through reading and discussion of appropriate articles or columns. A greater interest in leisure time activities on higher levels of enjoyment will be fostered through organized study of critical reviews of books, of concerts, of plays, of art exhibits.

These traits of wholesome character, good citizenship, open-mindedness, critical thinking, absence of prejudice, worthy use of leisure time, are not all that are implied in the workshop committee reports. They are, however, representative and the formulation of them in these reports is interesting evidence of the sanely progressive outlook of the experienced teachers who took part in the discussions.

II. The Background of Pupil Experience

Several of the workshop groups gave emphasis in their reports to the fact that newspaper reading is a vital factor in contemporary life. In the experience of a considerable segment of the population it is the only reading, save perhaps for an occasional periodical of the more popular type. The radio and the motion picture are the other sources of information, the agencies for the formation of opinions and attitudes.

Why emphasize so obvious a condition? Modern educational philosophy predicates that all school approaches must be based on pupil experience, and a school curriculum that neglects these three areas common to all pupil experience would be sterile and unproductive. We know that our procedure must be to help the pupil do in a somewhat better way the things that he would do of his own accord, anyway. To this end we use the newspaper, the radio, the motion picture, in the effort to have these agencies of learning used more intelligently, more effectively, with choice of material and program on a selective basis, guided by appreciation and good taste.

Intelligence in the choice of a newspaper becomes, therefore, a dominant objective. This choice, it is emphasized in all the reports, must be left to the pupil, not dictated by the teacher or the administrator; but the choice must not be haphazard. Standards for comparison and selection are set up by means of class discussion. Various criteria are suggested by the several groups, among them the following:

"The news should be unbiased and impartially presented"
(Group 2)

"Sensationalism and cheapness should be avoided" (Group 2)

"There should be a wide variety of special features"
(Group 2)

"Analyze various news articles on the same topic. Line up the
paper or the writer as to slant, if you can discover it. Does
the article present all the facts available? Compare same
news articles in different papers." (Group 5)

"How adequate is the coverage?" (Group 4)

"How superior is the English used?" (Group 4)

"Do headlines slant or color the news?" (Group 4)

"Consider the honesty of the advertising" (Group 4)

Other criteria included were the papers' attitudes towards
problems of social and civic import, whether impartial or
dictated by prejudices and political expediency; the dignity
of format; the fullness and timeliness of news coverage; the
number and ability of staff writers and special correspondents; the relative preponderance of text and illustrations as
an index to the level of intellectual appeal.

It has been the experience of all of us who have used
newspapers extensively in the classroom that guidance on the
basis of criteria such as these has led to thoughtful choice
on the part of the pupils—to an inevitable transition from
sensationalism, bias, and abbreviated news reports to the
dignity, the fearlessness, and the excellence of those papers
that have established the American tradition in news coverage and comment.

III. The Daily Paper as a Subject for Study

Scattered through the several reports are suggestions that
the newspaper itself, filling as large an area as it does in the
life of the community and of the individual, should be made
a topic of careful study. The various processes involved in

the production of the paper, the methods of organization, of selection of material to be published, of arrangement of sections and departments, as well as the more subtle considerations, such as attempts to influence opinion on other than editorial pages, are among the topics suggested for presentation to the pupils.

The suggestion, for example, is made in the report of Group 1 that a study of the credit labels to The Associated Press, The United Press, The International News Service, and similar organizations, lead to a study of the organization and functions of these services, and thus to an appreciation of the part played by them in furnishing timely and accurate information to the people, through their dailies. A realization of the stress laid, at the San Francisco conference, upon the vital importance of uninhibited access to the news by and from the peoples of all countries, would be a natural consequence of this study.

Group 2 would call the attention of the pupils to various other aspects of newspaper publishing. Mentioned specifically are the syndicated features, the photographs, and such special sections as sports pages and financial news. This group, too, urges a careful understanding by pupils of the difference between spot news and editorial comment, and of the newspaper ethics involved in keeping these areas distinct and separate.

This aspect of the newspaper referred to in the paragraph just preceding, the ethics of news publishing, is given especial emphasis in the report of Group 4. Here we have suggested an even more searching study of newspaper policy. It is urged by this group that among the topics to be considered in a close study of newspaper make-up there be included the placement of news items—the prominence given by one paper to various news stories or types of stories and the attitude of another paper as indicated by the placing of the material in a less prominent position. Headlines, according to this group, should be noted and compared. Are they a real index to the news story that follows? Are they so worded as to prejudge the content? Does the lead represent fairly both the headline and the factual content?

A careful study of editorials is included among the suggestions here. Mention is made of evidences of bias, but since the editorial is devoted to exposition and interpretation, it is difficult to see how bias can be avoided, or why. Opinion is the prerogative of the editorial column. The pupils, of course, should learn to distinguish between opinion based upon a fair consideration of all pertinent facts and evidence, and that engendered by prejudice.

Another item suggested for study and comparison is the use of photographs. How timely are they? To what interests and intellectual levels do they appeal? What degree of technical and dramatic excellence do they reach? While few pictures can reach the standards of emotional appeal attained by the Edward Rosenthal photograph of the flag-raising on Iwo Jima, many in our dignified papers are worthy examples of the photographer's ingenuity, his courage, and his art.

Although all groups consider the ethical standards of advertisement a fit topic for pupil study, this group urges a still further analysis as to dignity, arrangement, and artistic merit.

A further criterion, and one of exceptional importance, is the attitude of the various papers towards matters of social import, particularly in local community life. Campaigns for civic betterment—the methods of investigation and follow-up, are to be made matters of pupil interest and understanding.

Other items are included in other reports, such as a study of the format of the various papers, a consideration of the prominence and the reputation of the staff writers. Not all of the topics suggested could, of course, be considered at length by any one class in one term, but reference to the standards established must result in the end in wiser choice and deeper appreciation.

IV. The Daily Paper and the Start in Life

This function of newspaper study is implied to some extent in the reports of several groups, stated explicitly and emphasized in two. Guidance of pupil interests into fields of later activity and usefulness is accomplished, say these teachers, by classroom discussions of the achievements noted in the various fields of human endeavor—science, law, art, music, business enterprise. News items furnish highly vitalized and current information concerning opportunities in numerous professions and vocations, often are a guide to the preparation needed for success in these fields.

Various approaches are suggested: the study of newspaper biographies of successful men and women—even the obituary page is mentioned in this connection by one group —the keeping of scrapbooks and clipping collections classified according to the vocations being considered, a study of help wanted and situation wanted advertisements as an index to qualifications, opportunities, and remuneration to be expected, these and other procedures afford to the high school senior some opportunity to avoid the pitfalls of haphazard choice.

One interesting outcome of the study of the newspaper in secondary school not mentioned by any group but known to the writer through two instances, is the selection of journalism, itself, as a career.

V. The Newspaper and the Subject Areas

This is the topic dealt with primarily in earlier studies of the use of the newspaper in schools—in the two brochures, for example, published earlier by *The New York Times*. All the reports deal extensively with this area of discussion

—so much so that a cursive digest of the reports would extend this article far beyond the limits that are advisable. Some suggestions that seem most helpful are, accordingly, presented below in schematic outline, by quoting typical findings in the various reports. It is interesting to note that the daily paper has been found of value in subject areas that would hardly seem appropriate—stenography, typing, health education. Here an outstanding value becomes manifest. Much has been said of late of the "integration" of the various subject areas, of an elimination of the boundaries, entirely artificial and products of the schools and colleges, that separate English from the social studies, mathematics from science, and all from human life. Reaction against extreme views of the moderns in "progressive" education has emphasized the separateness of fields of learning, the need for considerable specialization in study if any degree of effectiveness is to be attained. Real integration becomes not an artificial fusion of discrete areas of subject matter, but an understanding of the inter-relations of disciplines and activities and the over-all unity of human experience.

As mentioned in an earlier paragraph, the common experiences of life furnish this integrating influence. For some, the instruments are books, travel, personal associations; for the large majority of our students they are the radio, the motion picture and, above all if wisely interpreted, the newspaper. Some indication of this unifying effect is apparent from a realization of the function of the daily paper in each of the areas included in the outline presented below.

English—

A rich source of informative material for oral and written English.

A source for current events discussions, forum discussions, debates, round table.

Study of critical reviews of plays, books, art exhibits.

A model for meaningful English expression.

A guide to current language usage.

An instrument for extension of vocabulary.

A supplementary text for reading and discussion.

A model for class and school publications.

A model for persuasive writing (editorials).

A model for exposition (editorials).

A study of letter-writing—analysis of letters from readers, incentive for writing letters to the editor.

Stimulation of interest in current literature.

Selection of a live spelling vocabulary.

Study of contemporary poetry.

The play—contemporary drama compared with earlier masterpieces.

The motion picture—critical evaluations—advantages and limitations.

The radio—reports of programs, newspaper listings, comparison of broadcasts with newspaper report and comment.

Mathematics—

The newspaper as a source of authentic material for problems —prices, stock quotations, volumes of imports and exports, graphs, batting and fielding averages, dimensions of areas, and a multitude of other items of mathematical significance.

The delivery and the distribution of the newspaper, the keeping of accounts, the payment of bills by check, handled as a student project affords valuable training in mathematics on a truly functional basis.

Study of advertisements gives real insight into comparative prices and values, budgeting income, and other aspects of consumer education.

Current practices and underlying philosophies relating to such topics as insurance, taxes, installment buying, simple and compound interest as related to investments, become real to pupils who learn to interpret newspaper accounts and reports in these fields.

The Social Studies—

It was in connection with the social studies, current events, history, geography, civics—that the use of newspapers in class first was emphasized. It is in this connection, perhaps, that the daily paper retains its primary importance. It is difficult to separate the various fields of the social studies, since they are closely interwoven in modern teaching.

History and Current Events—

The present as an outcome of the past—the continuity of history.

The past seen in terms of the present—historical cycles.

Contemporary happenings in the various news sections—foreign, national, local.

Evaluation of importance of news—advances in science, in human welfare, contrasted with the destruction caused by war, by selfish interests, by class conflicts.

Anniversaries as a stimulus to interest in the events that they commemorate.

Geography—

The life of the people of other lands in newspaper accounts of events and customs.

The meaning in human experience of earth features otherwise meaningless symbols on maps—rivers as highways or barriers, mountains as sources of mineral wealth and the accompanying human activities, climatic areas and the ingenuity of man in overcoming unfavorable climatic influences, and a host of other illustrations, gleaned from the news of the day, of the real meaning of geography as the study of the home of man, his activities and his industries.

The resources and the needs of nations—the functions of transportation, communication, exchange.

Places associated with current events—the maps of the war areas published by our great dailies.

The influence of climate and terrain on the progress of armies as well as on the activities of times of peace.

Civics and Citizenship—

The informed citizen.
The use and abuse of propaganda.
Other outcomes as listed in an earlier paragraph. (Character.)

Art—

Study of photographs and other illustrations.
Reports of exhibits.
Study of design in advertisements of clothing, houses, utensils.
The front page as a study in proportion, balance, emphasis.

Music—

Reports of concerts, operas.
Familiarity with achievements of contemporary composers
and performers.

Science—

The record of contemporary advances in all fields, military
and other.
Tables and daily reports—weather, tides.
News of science interests in special reports of meetings and
the like.
The implications of science in all the news of the day.
Illustrations in the news of principles of science studied from
experiment and abstract presentation in school.

Foreign Languages—

In Group 6 were several teachers of foreign languages in high
school.
They reported the very effective use of the daily paper in connection with several aspects of foreign language study.
Among the procedures listed were:
the constant use of the daily paper in connection with
studying the cultural and economic backgrounds of the
people whose language is being studied by the pupils—
social and political news, literary and artistic achievements;

the occasional use of foreign language newspapers published abroad for comparison with our native papers as to format, policies, types of news and other material presented;

the more frequent use of foreign language newspapers printed for circulation here, both those for the general reader, such as "Pour la Victoire" and those intended primarily for students, such as "Le Petit Journal."

Stenography and Typewriting—

The teachers of these subjects reported the daily paper as a very effective source of material for practice in dictation and transcription, not only enlivening drill periods through the use of meaningful content, but also emphasizing the inter-relations of these skill subjects with the topics and ideas germane to other subject areas.

Other subjects—

Various other fields of learning are represented in these reports. Thus, a teacher of printing has described the vitalizing of his subject by means of a talk on the production of a newspaper, the outcome of his own trip through the plant, and by the use of the newspaper to illustrate sizes and styles of type, spacing, layout, and kindred technical matters.

A teacher of dressmaking (Group 6) has used the daily paper extensively in having her pupils report on fashion trends, on the use of new materials, on consumer adaptation to wartime conditions, on requirements and opportunities in the textile industries, on the use of fashion pictures to stimulate creative expression and design.

VI. The Newspaper at Various Maturity Levels

Two of the workshop groups were composed entirely of teachers in the elementary grades, the first six years of school. An unexpected outcome of the discussions was the realization that even in the earliest years pupils may profit by an introduction to the daily paper—an acquaintance extending beyond the "comic strips." As the pupils grow older, more extensive use of the paper is made.

One third year teacher reports having the pupils study the maps in the papers and having her pupils associate the events of the day with the countries of their occurrence. Another teacher has her pupils adopt suitable words for conscious vocabulary enrichment, and use the pictures for oral language improvement through discussion. First and second year pupils have used the large print headlines to clip the separate letters and rearrange them in building new words, as their elders do in playing anagrams. The class bulletin board in all grades is enriched by the posting of clippings and pictures contributed by the pupils.

Development of good manners, of worthy civic attitudes, of respect for public property, are instanced by a teacher of the middle grades, in the report of Group 2, as outcomes of class use of the daily paper. Even in the lowest grades in many schools a class "newspaper" is printed on the blackboard by the teacher as items are dictated by the pupils. True, these items relate to intimate personal experiences of the pupils, but the display of the "grown-up" paper is a powerful stimulus to the efforts of the pupils in composing their own. It is an introduction to the most potent integrating influence of their school life in the twelve years ahead of them.

VII. THE ORGANIZED USE OF THE NEWSPAPER

Running through the comment of all the groups is the insistence that the use of the daily paper be not merely occasional, haphazard, but carefully planned and organized. System is introduced into the ordering of papers, the reception and distribution of the daily supply, the keeping of accounts, and, above all, the classroom techniques involved. These matters are discussed at some length in a brochure published by *The Times* several years ago. Briefly, the mechanical details when large numbers of newspapers are delivered daily, are taken care of by a newspaper squad, under the direction of a teacher assigned to the duty. It has been found, in a school using from twelve hundred to fifteen hundred copies daily, of two different papers, that the entire distribution by means of floor captains and helpers is accomplished during the twenty-minute interval between the entrance of the pupils and the beginning of the day's program.

In less favored neighborhoods, where expense is a consideration, each pupil subscribes for a copy one day in each week, all the pupils sharing the daily supply. In a few instances the teacher's single copy is made to serve the purpose.

Classroom technique for using the papers are many and varied.

They are used for silent reading, followed by discussion.

Clipping collections are organized and filed by topics.

Pupil scrap books are kept, containing clippings and appropriate pupil comment, a different area of the news being assigned to each pupil or pupil committee.

The pupils summarize the news for themselves at the end of the week, comparing their product with that appearing in the Sunday editions.

The paper is used to furnish models for composition exercises of all kinds, especially in classes that write their own occasional or periodical publications.

A topic for classroom or assembly discussion is announced a week or more in advance, and pupils search the paper for pertinent information to be used in debate.

Comparisons are made between radio news broadcasts and newspaper accounts, comparisons as to completeness, accuracy, fairness.

Many other methods and devices are included in the reports, and are indicated in foregoing sections of this summary.

To all of us who participated in the course, "The Newspaper, Its Making and Its Meaning," the experience has been one of pleasure and enlightenment. The able presentations made by members of *The Times* staff added greatly to our meager stock of knowledge concerning the organization and production of a great daily. Our contacts with personalities known to us in the past only by name were an added privilege and inspiration. Perhaps the deepest satisfaction to many of us has been the realization of the very wide extent to which progressive methods of education have become standard practice in our schools as a reinforcement, rather than a refutation, of philosophies and procedures that have come to us through many generations consecrated to the guidance of youth.

TEACHERS WHO HEADED THE WORKSHOP GROUPS

Ann Efros—P. S. 32, Manhattan
Lenore M. Haas—P. S. 119, Manhattan
Geraldine Saltzberg—James Monroe H. S.
Frank A. Smerling—Julia Richman H. S.
Marie G. Carrano—P. S. 85, Brooklyn
Margaret Michaelson—William H. Taft H. S.
Julius Laderburg—Horace Mann School
Robert H. Banker—P. S. 115, Manhattan
Louis Bach—New York School of Printing
Lillian Fassburg—Girls H. S.